MW01101885

Paper-son Poet

My Window of the World

Paper-son Poet

A multi-genre memoir by

Koon Woon

Goldfish Press, Seattle

Copyright 2016 by Koon Woon
All rights reserved

Goldfish Press, Seattle
2012 18th Avenue South
Seattle, WA 98144

Manufactured in the United States of America

ISBN - 13: 978-1530519484
ISBN - 10: 1530519489

Library of Congress Catalog Card Number: 2016938824

Cover and Book Design: Koon Woon

Photo credits: Frank Woon

Dedication:

This book is dedicated to Dr. Laurence P. Jacobs,

healer, mentor, and friend.

Contents

ACKNOWLEDGMENTS

This book is supported by a generous grant from the

City of Seattle's Office of Arts & Culture

With Special Thanks to Irene Gomez

Prologue:

The Seattle Chinatown Years (1985 – 2008)

Hing Hay Park

One of the places I have spent time orienting myself...

Locate yourself inside a seaport city
Locate yourself inside the inner city
Locate yourself inside a small square
Locate yourself inside you
this is you

You are the dragon on the wall
You are the railroad when America was young
You are the immigrant hands that lay the track
you are here
it is you

This is a place where you come to
This is a place within you
You were here when the sky was born
you are here
you are you

America I have no other place to go now
But to go within myself and find all that is still new
This is too a place for you as well as for me
you and I are both here
we are here

Of all the places where I have spent my time
Of all the places that have bruised my heart
America you are deep within my heart now
The pain was enormous
yes, it was you

Now don't tell me now to go back
Back to Wales or to Bavaria
America I am now a Native as any Native can be
to have withstood the pain
and yet still be free..

Instructions for immigration interrogation:

This was the final step, to be "interviewed" at the American Embassy in Victoria, Hong Kong in 1960. Success would enable me to immigrate to the US to rejoin my parents and the rest of my family.

Third Auntie and I rode the ferry from the Kowloon peninsula across the Hong Kong harbor to the island of Victoria, the administrative seat of Hong Kong and the surrounding territory that were ceded to the British at the conclusion of the Opium Wars. The embassies were all on Victoria.

"You will not say she is your grandmother. She's an old woman who came to live with you and you were told to call her 'Grandmother,'" Third Auntie instructed me. I nodded while I watched the water churned behind the boat.

"Does China have anything as modern and nice as this?" Third Auntie asked about the comfort of the ferry boat. She knew full well that China did not at the time, as she herself came to Hong Kong just two years earlier with her two children. She will be going to Kingston, Ontario in Canada later to rejoin her husband.

"No, Auntie Siem," I replied to her, "but China will some day." This ferry was actually a marvel, as I came from the village where we did not have electricity, running water, or even a bicycle. I reflected about having been born in a timeless village:

No prophet can live in your village, which faces East like a sunflower and as it turned, ends up facing West. You seldom ate three meals a day but sometimes you ate as many as five. On those occasions the water-buffalo grazed on the perimeters of the village pond, which years later, in America, you estimate it to have the dimensions of a high school football field.

Then a young woman came home to you and the old woman whom you called "Grandmother." She had just fired a rifle with other village boys and girls who heard the shots from the Korean War reverberate from the village walls with slogans denouncing US Imperialism. Chairman Mao's son was shot down and someone from our village went to the front. The scars from the Japanese bombings in the Sino-Japan War left deep holes in the village yard. The bombed houses were never rebuilt. I was not yet born. Grandmother told me as I was preparing arrowroot starch with her in our village home that my father was that year thirty-seven.

"Your father is so tall that he had to lower his head when entering a room," my Grandmother said. Now I was suddenly nine years old and we were leaving the village forever, leaving that teenage girl behind.

It was the year 1958. We arrived in Canton after a journey on yellow water. A hundred years before my birth we vanquished the English here when they imposed opium. They went up to Nanking however and subdued the decadent Empress, who then ordered Canton to desist. For the next decade my ancestors were lured by the gold dust of Californ. They were "indentured servants" who built the railroads in Western United States. They hung like a basket of sorrow when dangling from a mountain to chisel the mountainside. They dynamited tunnels through mountains to give dragons a path and they linked up with the Irish who were advancing from the East. Those who were sick, too sick to work, were unceremoniously tossed from the mountain. There was only so much food.

They come at me with hatchets:

I had no memory of my father who was in the US then. I was eleven and China was under Communism. I often imagined what my father was like. But I could only do it with the tools and knowledge I had. I kept having this horrendous nightmare that my father is really a vampire, the lead vampire and I was infected! In the village we attend Party meetings and toil in the rice paddies but when we sleep, our bodies open with a thousand sores, and we need blood to coat our sores. Nowhere is this found in Party Literature and we are forbidden to speak, write or even think of it.

At day, everyone greet us deferentially, but it is only due to the fact that the Party had appointed us, and if they know that we suck their blood with our phantom proboscis while they sleep, they would tear us apart limb by limb.

In the morning everyone wakes with a sense of violation. They have been drained of their blood and robbed of their strength. This is the way we collect "taxes" for the Party, and one may call it the Old-Fashioned Way, the way that cannot be told, but the way that is the way…

My father orders me never to tell. When by chance his mosquito avatar meets with mine sucking the same victim, he gives me the skull and he takes the thigh. "I get the fat and you get the bone," he says. I oblige because I am a dutiful son. I help my father plant rice as well as harvest it in the rice paddies. But we are not fat from rice; we are fat from others' blood. If they know that I am writing this down, the victims and even my father would come at me in the daylight with hatchets…

How it began:

"The Tao that can be told is not the Tao.
The name that can be named is not the name."

- Tao Te Ching

Memoir one day in the village:

Marcel Proust would like the timelessness of our village. In winters, we wear all our day-time clothes including the cotton jacket, and snuggle under several layers of blankets. I slept with my grandmother, two human engines. It only froze once in the nine years that I remember in our village. People collected ice and put it into glass jars believing that the water would cure fevers. Our house is unheated as all the houses in the village were not, and so it was cold at night exacerbated by the few calories that we consume because food was not as plentiful in winter, and in-between meals I always thought of food. In the morning though we stayed in bed until the sun shone on the village yard, the children would huddle against a wall to receive the warmth of the sun. We smiled. We used small stones to play jacks.

Our very own rooster crows in the utility room of our village duplex shared with Uncle Harry's mother. Grandmother always had me sleep in the inside of the bed next to the wall, in fear of my rolling off the bed. Daybreak. Grandmother and I get out of bed. We had a mosquito net over our bed but my adopted sister Ah Deel doesn't. Ah Deel's bed is just two planks over two wooden horses, and the fondest memories I have of her bed is that a couple of neighbor kids, Ah Deel, and I would play card games while sitting on her bed, and the game we played the most was "Old Maid." Ah Deel's bed is by the window, the only window of the long bedroom with an attic that we stored old items. The window has wooden shutters and two iron bars.

Grandmother heats water with the wood stove in our dirt-floor kitchen for me to wash my face with a facial towel. I asked Ah Deel why she doesn't use warm water instead of cold water to wash her face. She said that it would wrinkle her skin. Now I know that it costs money to buy wood for fire. And that's why neither Grandmother nor Ah Deel uses heated water. In the same way, they wash their feet at night with cold water, while I have warm water, and this was all before I was nine-years old. When I was nine, Grandmother and I went to Canton and left Ah Deel all alone in the house, and she was only seventeen.

I loved to play cards, and my favorite game was 13-cards and poker. In 13-cards you are to make a head, a middle, and a tail with 3, 5, and 5 cards in that order by increasing strengths, according to poker hand rules. And of course up to four players can play this game. I was extremely good at poker and not only did I become the best poker player in my village but also the best card shark in my primary school. The teachers confiscated my deck of cards. I refused to go to school and spend two weeks fishing while school was in session. Ah Deel never told Grandmother, and finally she related word to me that the teachers would give me back my deck of cards. I went back to school to receive it and then they told me I cannot play cards at school, and by then, fishing alone for six hours a day was getting old, because I could not give my catch to grandmother. And I missed my friends at school and so I stopped playing cards.

I have a scar above my left eye. I was told I was hit by a swing. Ah Deel was supposedly taking care of me and she was on the swing when I got too close and the swing hit me on my eye. I was two and Ah Deel was only eleven. She did not know what to do but to try to wash the blood in the lotus pond. No doubt she was panicking. Uncle Harry's mother was walking near and she saw what happened and she slapped Ah Deel for her carelessness. Grandmother told me that my eye was shut for days and she was afraid that I lose vision. But it did not damage any nerves or the eye itself. In fact, I can see better with my left eye than my right today. Ah Deel, however, was deeply hurt and angered that a neighbor not related to her slapped her. I of course have no memory of this at all.

I was told that Ah Deel came to our home with her grandmother. It is said that Ah Deel's parents were killed in the Japanese invasion. Her grandmother took Ah Deel to my Grandmother, after she had inquired in my village who was the best prospect to leave her granddaughter. Everyone pointed out my grandmother and the fact that my parents were overseas, so that they will be a source of money.

"I am an old woman and this is my granddaughter. I cannot take care of her much longer. Please show mercy and take her in, even as a servant," Ah Deel's grandmother supposedly thus beseeched my grandmother, and my grandmother said that she needed a younger helper, being old herself. So, Ah Deel came to stay with us. But I do not know for sure. And when my parents later called me a communist son, I knew less how Ah Deel is related to me. Is she my mother's illegitimate child, the result of unfaithfulness? Or was she the result of rape, by a Japanese soldier or a Chinese communist cadre? The "shame" of being a servant girl really upset Ah Deel. Grandmother treated her as a granddaughter, and we paid for her school tuition. And during the years of the Korean War, Ah Deel, though a teenager at fourteen, was active in the village militia. She was deeply ashamed and angered of called a servant girl and slapped by Uncle Harry's mother. And it is to my disservice that after I left China, I did not think of Ah

Deel, and she was never spoken of in our family. Is there some skeleton in the closet?

First cigarette:

There are things you rather not think about now. The time you were drowning in the village pond. Actually you recall it was three times maybe that you were fished semi-conscious out of the shallow end of the pond by older boys. The sneaky suspicion is that they had tossed you in.

But the same young boys in the village took me at age 9 to climb a tree when it lightly rained in the village. We leaned against a limb of the tree while standing in its crotch and lit cigarettes and smoked it with the burning end in the mouth.

How can I know?

How do I know what I am about to tell you? By taking a course in epistemology? I don't know for certain. Mostly it is what my mother tells me and what my father sometimes tells me at the closing of the restaurant in the wee hours of the morn, when we hear the Georgia-Pacific freight train rattled by Bay Avenue in the West End in Aberdeen in Washington State whistling a forlorn tune. And here is how it began:

It began ominously. When I was a boy in China during the time of the Korean War, my grandmother and my Uncle Chay took me to the village cemetery to an empty grave. They spoke in hushed tones but within my earshot. I did not know what they were saying. I gathered that someone should have been buried in the empty grave along with all our deceased relatives in the Lock village named Nan On, meaning Southern Peace. I was about five or six years old. But this story actually began almost one hundred years earlier with my great grandfather's sojourns in the United States. He had been a "piggy guest," as we Chinese say, meaning that he was an "indentured servant," was to work in America for 30 years and was not allowed to marry a white woman, nor to vote, nor to testify against a white person in court.

At the time of the California Gold Rush in 1849 (exactly one hundred years before I was born), in China, we were fighting excruciating hunger and dirty wars. Brigands had taken what rice we have after the War Lords extorted their shares. We starved along with the monks in autumn when the rice crops were devastated by locusts. Our bonds to the land were thus severed by Heaven. We indentured ourselves at the docks for 300 gold pieces for our families we leave behind. We became piggy-guests to America. Whether we can come back to see our loved-ones alive or dead was again an issue Heaven decides.

The Last Chess Game

Irene my love imagine every time I move a pawn,
You fill the grocery cart with ham and yams, peas and corn.

Every time I move a bishop or a knight,
The radio changes its tunes and new stars are born

In other galaxies, and when I move a castle,
Half of the real estate in this town are transferred to Asians.

And if I move my Queen, honey you'd nudge me in my arm,
And the other guy will not get a check or a mate,

But he would fumble for his cancer sticks, swallow too much espresso
And drop dead in his gigolo shoes.

Because of the way I am, the way I had to live, and the way I play, honey,
Every game is my last, and all my life honey,

I have avoided creams and starches, sugar and gods, honey,
All my life I try to do just this -

To make a feeling with you last -
So that each time I befriend, oppose, unfold, or behead an opponent,

It is for you, my dearest. I have played so many "my last" games, honey,
I am as dangerous but as secure as a nuclear arsenal.

But now you are firmly at my side, I will pawn the chess board for a cup of tea,
And turn to an infinite better study - you and poetry!

My very first impression of the United States:

Far Apart

The first thing I noticed is how far apart the houses were. I thought they must not like each other in America, to live so far apart. That feeling became even more pronounced as my father drove between towns on the high way. Even though my parents were speaking in Chinese to me, they seem very familiar and yet very distant. My siblings were all excited to see their oldest brother from China, though they did not largely comprehend what my parents were asking me. Is the jade secured? Are the gold pieces sewn into your pants? It was my one and only time as a smuggler. My parents had borrowed money for my air fare, and that was to pay for my passage here.

It was on October 31, 1960 that my plane landed at Sea-Tac airport in Washington State. I boarded the plane alone in Hong Kong. An hour or so later I was at Taipei, and shortly a few hours later I was in Tokyo. There we had dinner. I dined alone on fried chicken and orange juice, but all I could ingest was the orange juice. It was the first flight for me and it was the first time I saw snow, far away in the distance on top of Mount Fuji.

I remember the airline stewardess telling me when to get back on the plane, but I forgot the plane's flight number, and I didn't know how to read the tote board because it was in Japanese and English. I nearly panicked. Despite my confusion, my wits prevailed and I flagged down a man who seemed to work at the airport. I wrote in Chinese that I wanted to go to America. Fortunately, he could read Chinese, for the Japanese had borrowed from the Chinese culture at one time. He told me the time and flight time, and a few minutes later, I got back onboard.

The Matrix - first consciousness

We owe our consciousness to the movie The Matrix, which is dramatization of Rene Descartes' Fifth Meditation, which says in effect: "What if, while you were asleep, an Evil Genius has changed the world, how would you know when you wake up?"

Koon Woon, you woke up with a White identity, in Plato's Cave perhaps but with all the "shoot them up bang-bang" philosophies of Western Civilization, up to the latest theories and modes of deconstruction? It seems like you have been here before? Load yourself back up to the computer - The Matrix. It seems that you had dreamt you were Chinese once upon a time, even studied the rudimentary Chinese language and demanded Chinese food for most of your meals and even thought that Chinese girls were beautiful. Now you longed for a long-legged blonde, as the song laments: "It takes a long-handed shovel to dig a deep, wide hole; yes, it takes a long-handed shovel to dig a deep, wide hole; but it takes a long-legged woman to satisfy my soul."

The people in Seattle Chinatown, and there are broadly speaking, two classes of them - one, the recent immigrants who work and live here, and find all their entertainment in gambling clubs and an occasional trip to the whorehouse. Where is the whorehouse? They give you an address and call a cab for you when you emerge the big winner in a mahjong game. Those girls will only be town for a few days before they "fly to accept their nursing assignment in another city." They are only nurses moonlighting. Anyway, no matter what is your illness, they can make you feel better.

The other class of people are the businessmen. They have nice homes in Bellevue and Redmond. They will be long-gone when the crimes begin for the night in Chinatown. They are only interested in counting money. There is something magical about money. You can have your son's high school grades *enhanced* by a gift to the school administrator. It helps to have an Asian on the Board of the Public Schools. Share and share alike, everybody benefits in the school system administration. You been to Canton or Guangzhou as it is called now? If the light is yellow we go through, and if the light is red, we go around it. Chinese have been inventive people for thousands of years, and they have invented things like the iron and wood plow, paper to write your novels or to print them out, gun powder to make money for the Wah Ching and for the reservations in terms of illegal fireworks, and mostly, they invented the compass that enabled Christopher Columbus to "discover" America. And so here we are: big fish eat small fish, and big dog rules little dog.

Here in the Chinatown Matrix is the Chinese Seattle Post and the International Examiner. Actually they should be classified as fiction magazines.

At a Chinatown Monastery:

A woman is reading a telephone book upside down as she tosses poker chips into variously colored bins. The crisp sounds of hard plastic colliding with steel boxes ring out from the last tenement room in the corner of the corner building next to the I-5 Freeway. These maroon and gray buildings are waiting to be moved like rooks and bishops to another sector of the real estate chessboard. The players are unseen but are nevertheless real, as real as the dead mouse on the staircase. When noises die down, the mice come out in *this* man's room and he studies the bag of rice as he would try to memorize selections of the US Constitution for a practical end. But the despair of citizenship make men created unequal but they are each guaranteed to pursue happiness.

So, the Abbot is in his monastic room in deep meditation. Before long, two dragons will peer into this room. The Abbot's sword is ready…

But what is the Abbot trying to achieve? He is going to pull me out of the Matrix. I am still Chinese. He is going to pull me out of the Matrix.

"Isn't it obvious that you are Chinese," you say. "It's in your genes. The way you look and where you came from and what you call yourself."

No, I am Chinese because I am not readily accepted for my genes, the way I look and where I come from. Being Chinese then is what I am not, and not for what I am.

I wish I was not Chinese the way you are not American, or White, or Black, or a Policeman, or a Criminal, or a Con Artist, or a Scholar, or a Heavy Laborer. Then, everyone is the same?

Same my ass, shame on your ass.

These little Chinatowns, always in the old urban areas, where people born, live, work, and die within a few city blocks whether it is San Francisco, or New York, or Seattle or Boston, where the façade is reminiscent of imperial China with stinking garbage in the back of so many restaurants, teashops, and cafes. It is a microcosm of China - bittersweet memories of the land these Overseas Chinese left, and the non-acceptance of life in America to be so relegated to the inner city with plastic and neon glitter. While the children hide from commerce with their grandmothers in the tenements above the Chinatown shops. They resemble house-arrests or minimal security prisons. ***We found that America is the land of prisons, and that is why I am Chinese.***

I took a little jaunt in Chinatown Seattle early in the morning at 10 AM when all the banks open. I realize that there are more banks per acre in Chinatown than anywhere else in the city, including the financial district. I then realize how big gambling, possibly billions are transacted in Chinatown and millions are laundered daily through the restaurants and certain gift shops that no one visits.

In the news, the China police busted a gambling ring worth 68 billion dollars of Internet betting from betters mainly on the Mainland but the betting centers were in Hong Kong and Taiwan

"The Tao that can be told is not the Tao.
The name that can be named is not the name."

- Tao Te Ching.

Great-Grandfather:

Year of arrival - circa 1880. Year of death and burial --- 1929 atop Queen Anne Hill in Mount Pleasant Cemetery in Seattle. His name was Lock Li and it meant a "heavy metal" in Chinese. My great-grandfather was the first of the Locks to come. He operated a laundry and had shares in a restaurant. His English was surprisingly good. So the mayor of Hoquiam used him as a labor contractor and together they went to the Lock villages in our county of Toishan to conscript five-hundred men to come to work on the railroads in Humptulips, north of Hoquiam in Washington State. One of these men was the grandfather of Gary Locke (who anglicized his name). Gary was the first Chinese governor in the USA and served two terms as Governor of Washington State, the US Secretary of Commerce, and finally Ambassador to China.

The gold dust of Californ, Gimshan it was, or Golden Mountain, had lured my ancestors to this America, but they largely came too late, and had to eat their "bitter strength (coolie)" by dynamiting tunnels in granite to make path for the mechanical dragon, the locomotive. Or, to hang from baskets on the cliffs and chisel a roadway for the train. If they got sick, they were tossed off the mountain because food is only limited to those who can work. Even at that, that was a good time, because they got paid and were able to send money to loved ones in the old country. The family structures or what's mistakenly thought of as criminal organizations, the Tongs, enable them to survive with mutual help. But when mining and railroad building came to a halt, "The Chinese Must Go!" became the slogan.

For almost a hundred years yet I was still not born. And I did not learn of this until my psychiatrist told me. He is of Irish descent. They had faced similar discrimination. "The Irish Needn't Apply" signs at shops that were hiring. "Men of respect" from other places were given a shovel to dig and slept back to back with their wives because they couldn't afford another *Bambino.* A nation of immigrants meant centuries of oppression for some. I needn't tell you of those who came *involuntarily* or those who never come by boat - Afro-Americans and the Native Americans. Let's watch television tonight and fornicate to forget these chapters of history.

A Childhood Incident:

I was cleaning clams under the cold faucet. I used a parry knife to pry the clam from its shell and cut open the innards with a pair of scissor and rinse away the gut under the stream of cold water which got colder and colder under I was working with numb hands. After doing 10 limits of 18 clams apiece, I couldn't fit them all into a gallon jar. And my brother John runs into the house through the backdoor just then.

"Hobart is beating up Jack and he has a knife!" Jack is another brother.

"Damn it, you go and help him!"

John went out as I put away the kitchenware. Later he comes back and said that Hobart and his brothers and a couple of other guys were there. So I went out to see what the ruckus was all about.

I faced Hobart and his two brothers and their two friends. "You guys are out of line," I said, we are only playing in our backyard.

"Your brother said something nasty about my sister!" Hobart yelled.

"Come on, Hobart," I said, "put that knife away. You know your sister Rayleen likes Jack."

I suddenly realized that one of Hobart's friends likes his sister and was going to squeeze Jack out. So I said to John, "Go home and get the big butcher knife."

"You mean the real big knife?" John asked, somewhat fearful this was going to escalate.

"Yeah, bring the biggest knife your eyes can see!"

A little later I have the butcher knife in hand. I said mockingly toward Hobart, "Hobart wants to fight but Hobart has a smaller knife; Hobart has a small butter knife."

A tense moment went by and I had even forgotten to look at Jack, the alleged precipice of all of this commotion. Hobart tossed his knife in the ground and I threw the butcher knife a distance where no one was standing. Hobart and I shook hands. And he said, "I am protecting my sister."

I nodded and said, "I am protecting my brother. No arguments, right?"

"No, none," he said and took his entourage of brothers and friends toward their house on the other end of the housing project in West End.

The Next Town:

Time it was 1962 near the Hoquiam River where pale lights of the taverns were burning in the low-blood-sugared afternoons when Hank and I climbed the dimly-lit stairs of the Emerson Hotel to Uncle Harry's room on the third floor. On the third round of knocking we'd hear the bed creak and Uncle Harry would open the door ajar in his short and thin frame, naked except a yellowed brief, smelling like the beer bottles with slugs inside that Hank would find at the end of Oak Street. I'd say, "Uncle Harry, it is time to open the restaurant now."

And Uncle Harry said, "OK, boys, I will be right there."

And seeing how small the hotel room is, I thought of the beetles I used to catch and kept them in match boxes. Uncle Harry only needed a room of his own in America. All his meals were eaten at the café.

In the village in China, my grandmother, my adopted sister and I shared a duplex with Uncle Harry's mother. When I was more grown up, my father told me that as a young man, Uncle Harry had ardently wooed his wife-to-be. But his mother had objected to his choice. Uncle Harry then purchased a pistol and chased the old woman through the village yards until she urinated on herself out of fright. Uncle Harry then got his wish and now he is waiting for Immigration to let his wife and son to leave Hong Kong.

My father frequently bailed Uncle Harry out of jail, and knowing the other's loneliness, my father said, "He doesn't have a family to go back to after work. He goes back to his room and faces the four walls like a crazy man, and that's why he drinks, and so often drinks himself into puke on the street."

Our family was all here now in Aberdeen. We lived in the housing project with a family of nine divided into three bedrooms. I was told later Uncle Harry thought of the café partnership with my father was unfair and business was scant. "Whatever profit there is, you get it all," said Uncle Harry to my dad, "your children's cheeks are rosy and fat." Soon after, the restaurant went out of business.

I've told you the fragility of my love...

I've told you of the fragility of my love,
and yet how it endures like a leaf pressed into a book,
how the pain and how inappropriately the hate,
like the Nagasaki and Hiroshima bombs
left a silence whereof no man can speak…
It is this that is the fragility of my love,

knowing my awareness is pain; I leave you in my mind
the many times I think of the silence
wherein my mother's voice should drone, but
the gentle hands released me to bed where the smell of
kerosene from the village lamp burnt past the hour of moths
when we shut the window to village crickets,
when the tender bamboo shoots, their new fragile leaves
bud in the fragility of my love for you,
as I want to travel blind with you as far into the night
until the sun rises in Japan, and I will sail my junk
into phantom waters. Yet, my love endures
like cloth flapping in the wind

Uncle Sum:

It began when I was walking bare-footed on the hot stone slabs, half-way to my Uncle Sum's house in my mother's village Bow-Lung. The stones would heat the air and as the air rose it distorted the view in the distance, and so I kept seeing images of my childhood friend Gan. I was hoping against hope. I knew he had been "adopted out" for a sum of money given to his mother for "milk" she raised him with from her teats. I overheard the older people say that he had been given to a couple who had no children. Also, they said that Gan has to go to some place far away so that he will never be able to remember his way "home."

My village was named Nanon, meaning "South Peace." Everyone in the village is surnamed Lock, as it is patriarchal and part of the three villages of the Lock clan. I was at this time around seven years old and Grandmother took care of me. I had an "adopted sister" too named Ah Deel. Ah Deel came to live with us when I was two. That was what I was told.

I don't today, at age sixty-six, believe anything much anymore. I just want to tell the reader that I have suffered two-thirds of my life with schizoaffective mental illness, and my village years, though hard and unforgiving, was what enabled me to survive my prolonged illness. And it is not only the mental illness, it is also how other people misunderstand and are sometimes cruel to you if you are different. Yes, I would fit the bill in today's culture of "political correctness." I am "Asian, immigrant, and disabled," and elderly now and low-income. This qualifies me to Medicaid, SSI, and low-income public housing and an allotment of food stamps. I am telling you that I live like a King in the Middle Ages and comparing my early life in the village, I would have lived like an emperor in China's long illustrious but also sad history.

Before we dive into my story, let's have a pot of tea. We are at the coffeehouse named The Last Exit on Brooklyn in Seattle's U-District. Here is where I honed my wits on chess and Go, studied math and counter-culture in the late 60s and early 70s, reading Collin Wilson's The Outsider and R.D. Laing's The Politics of Experience. And people extolled the virtues of the Dali Lama, as if I, being Chinese, am the barbarians that China have come to be to overrun a peaceful and beautiful Tibetan culture, expelling the very leader of TRUE Buddhism. You can quit reading now, if you want, and take a walk in Seattle's rain. Yes, take a walk in the rain first and then come back, my story will resume.

I face the problem now of what to include and what to leave out in my narrative as memory is selective and history depends on the "historian's" version of it. If you had been in my life, even tangentially, I apologize for leaving you out if I do so, for I have learned from you, good or bad, for it is only a human experience. I am the seeker of the Tao and if I ever find it, it will just as soon be forgotten because that is the nature of the Tao. If I have inconvenienced you or harmed you in anyway, I now ask for forgiveness. I also ask for forgiveness of not reaching out to you.

(Song of the Village)

In Water Buffalo time:

The water buffalo is a black boulder around which white
Butterflies flit, controlling the image of my village.
It is four pillars holding up a shrine topped by Attila's head.
Slapping its paintbrush tail, sure-footed, it advances
Slowly, not impressed by dynastic inventions of paper,
compass,
and gunpowder,
Not by imperial vassals intoxicating concubines with plum
wine.
This working philosophic benign beast of the East, a prince
Meditating on plum blossoms while the kingdom is overrun
By brigands no different than soldiers.
It sinks its head into the grass on the perimeter of the village
Pond where daggers of carp and dace rip his shadow on the
water,
Where black shrimp and loaches scout the bottom
And snails cling to slate banks.

In earliest mornings, I woke to the village dialect jostling
In my head like cauliflowers sizzling in sesame oil
In the wok, like chatty sparrows in the yung tree,
Like cicadas in bamboo groves, like buckets splashing
Into the village well. I heard the drinking song of the men
In the village yard the night before. With bamboo pipes
And a bucket of rice wine, they had sung.

"Heavy, heavy, the dew lies over the clovers.
Bring, bring out flasks of silver.
Merry, merry under a dome of stars.
But soon, too soon this night will be over..."

Voices taut, frog drums deep as rice paddies.
But I dreamt a deeper voice, my father's pales in comparison.
It's hinted by Gungfu drums, bellow of water buffalo, a racine fissure.
It was as proclaimed by Lu Hsun, "In the stillness of mountains,
Hear the peal of thunder." But when I woke, the dew was gone.
A shaft of sunlight fell on my childhood slate.

My sister renews the Ming vase with fresh pussy-willows.
Grandmother steams rice, and the chicken sits on a new egg.
I drink tea from the spout while my sister redoes my shoelaces.
Off to school 3 li away, trotting on village pond banks
And collecting schoolmates in the morning haze.
When I see a water snake swimming on the lotus pond,
I déjà vu Narcissus lost his life. His gifts came early
And ours not at all. We are the contingent of zodiac animals
Off to seek Buddha: the horse, the rabbit, the tiger, the rooster...
The ox trots out first, faithful, steadfast, but when he
Arrives, the rat on his back jumps off
And gets to Buddha first.

I often meditate at the pond near the school,
Watching the soft, thin legs of the praying mantis
Subdue a bug in full armor, seeing it as the monks did
In Shaolin Temple 500 years before. Other masters studied
The movements of cranes, eagles, and birds fighting with

snakes.
Li Po, our legendary poet, in 700 A.D., perfected
The Drunkard's Style of Kung-fu, which bewilders
The opponent with fluid but erratic movements.

When my little friends mocked me for my seriousness,
Our teacher, under the shade of the Yung tree bursting with berries,
Told us Mencius had dreamed he was a butterfly
Dreaming it was a man. I was confused, in a house
Of mirrors, and thought existence is mutual illusion.
Would I cease to exist if I didn't think of my dog
Who thinks of me? My little friends made faces at me.

New Year comes to the village banging a gong
And exploding demon-chasing firecrackers. And lucky money.
But the village recedes away like the galaxies. In these
Thirty years what will not change in form or utility
Except art for its own sake?
Heraclitus says I can't cross the same river twice.
Einstein says if I must I can go to the future, but never to the past.
But surely as long as one water buffalo is fanned by
The evening breeze, the village is there like the smile of the Cheshire Cat
And exists in the Platonic world; all else is an approximation.

Sunflowers, yellow and white chrysanthemums, lychees,
Girls' red cheeks, dew-moist winter-melon little buddhas
In the gardens. Robins, beetles, and cicadas sing my way
To my uncle's village. He rises and his wife burns incense.
He clears the abacus with one motion and teaches me the rhymes
One chants to enable the fingers to go faster than the brain.

He is a wine merchant steeped in Confucius.
Where would a woman wash her husband's clothes
If not at the river by the ancestral shrine?
What part of the chicken to give to the nephew if not the drumstick?
And how else to measure but by exact yards and inches?
He has many children but there is no unnecessary noise.

I forage the pine hills behind his house as a bandit.
The turpentine from the virgin pines makes me dizzy.
The wood is kept as furniture for newlyweds.
I play until I fear real bandits will come
When the sky is devout with thousands of incense tips.

But surely memory is selective. I don't remember not having
My mother's milk, only the quarrels with village women
My mother's age. I don't remember three generations of a family
Taken by dysentery, just the bitter cod liver oil
My grandmother spooned me.
I don't remember my cold little toe except that cloth was allotted
Only once a year, and only in black or blue.
I don't remember famines, just the human chain formed
To relay water to the stricken rice paddies,
Where the leeches had dehydrated.

Still, village girls marry as soon as the dew evaporates
From the corn. The mulberry was for jumping into the village pond.
What China had, we had. And when it was all quiet,
The sunflowers so turned. The papayas got fat and golden,
And peasants trotted out with hoes and straw hats.
It is quiet in the garden where I fish in the pond.
Peas incubate in pods, the lettuce full and clean,

And ladybugs monitor the gardens
To make sure this is the order of things
Before the invention of mail delivery.

In the semi-tropical evening, pink clouds race and diffuse
Like the colors and textures of my jade bracelet.
The water buffalo is led into the dusty village yard,
Mud-caked on its loins, distracted by my dog cutting
Across its path. He collects his primeval motions into shape,
Shakes his Hegelian head, exhales, slaps his paintbrush tail,
Lapses into a revelry, and goes into internal monologue:

O beast I am, humble beast.
Some man, he must have been an emperor,
Or the son of such an emperor, said, "The Original Son
Is the mother of the universe, the sword that divines light
From chaos, the mother of all things..."
The sun atop the tree is East.
The mountains seek comfort in the hills, the hills seek
Rest in the valleys, and the valleys beget rivers.
The mountain cat descends into the lowlands
And the field mice look up for hawks
And the darkening earth looks for the moon...

And loving the grasses as I have for thirty years,
First owned by one man, then by his son,
While the mountains are unvarying,
With mud caked on my loins, trudging the maze of rice fields,
A black dot against unvarying mountains,
The soil furls, my eyebrows moisten, the bittersweet song
Of my master, himself deep in mud, the fury of work,
Calculating how many bowls of rice the harvest will give.

A beast is not able to calculate mous, catties, and grains.
Work begins when the monsoons recede. In the evening,
When I am sufficiently grazed, I sink into the village pond

And drop dung for black shrimp...

Yet a man, with all his skill on an abacus, is afraid
Of things he cannot see. The man and his family
Are afraid of dark, gloomy gods handed down to them
And buy copious amounts of incense and charms.
My mother, whose teats I suckled for only a brief while,
Gave me no such gods of thunder to fear.

I don't even fear tigers. A man is cursed with worry:
Thieves because he has too much, fires because he is careless,
And ghosts because he offends others.
But I, with the gold-pleated sky for a blanket,
Sweet-smelling rice straw for a bed, a breeze from the river,
I have recompense for my toil, with the village symphony
Of crickets, cicadas, and bullfrogs,
I shall say beasthood is as good as Buddhahood.

I conjecture a water buffalo constellation in another galaxy,
A real spirit, not a tattered array of dying stars,
A form but not only a form.
Up in heaven, my soul-mate has no ring pierced
Through his elegant nose and no harness to shackle him down.
And here below, if beasts can speak, we will form quorums
And overthrow empires by a conspiracy of tails.

But alas, nature gives us no such voice or equipment
Just a reluctant compliance to serve.
Though our masters in turn fear the tax collectors,
It is we who are sold, exchanged, or placed on the chopping block.
We do not think? No!
Our lack is that our intelligence is not equal to our strength.

The beast is weary, is led by a boy to a bed of straw.
Inside our house, in the kerosene lamplight,
My sister undoes her ponytail, which a while ago was a bowstring

Back from a political meeting, she says tractors will come
To our village. When electric lamps light up the village yard,
She says, ghosts will be gone.
Grandmother, with her feet bound in the last dynasty, will
see
New light with her old eyes.
She gives me crackers and tea, and draws the mosquito net.
I hear a faint moan from the water buffalo.
He too will be liberated.
Though the past is solipsistic, its existence requiring
A mind to behold it, childhood writes indelibly
A million dollar check into life.
Dragonflies hover over chrysanthemums
Like helicopters over a burning forest.
Bananas and grapes bunch together like families.
Women splash buckets into the well.
I look for the faint prints of water buffalo.
The water buffalo got old and died.
It was shared by the whole village,
Lucky money for a calf conscripted.
A sad note crept into the men's drinking songs,
But not for long, with rice wine they sang
Again of subduing tigers and the various calamities
From the beginning of time.
On my childhood slate were drawings of chickens,
mulberries,
And numerals from Arabia.
Then I learned how to write the characters "water buffalo."

A Day in the #317 Tenement Room:

The weather has nothing to do with it, but it was hot in Seattle. A half mile down the hill from Harborview Medical Center lies the gray and rusting buildings of Chinatown Seattle. Jackson Street, the main thoroughfare, runs down to the water of the Elliott Bay. Bracketed by little Saigon up East and Yester Terrace to the North lie this prime real estate that the downtown people want to usurp and expand down south where it is the home of the sports stadiums, which, on game days, congest the already congested Chinatown streets. Merchants complain because there is not enough parking as it is without the incursion of game goers who don't patronize the Chinatown shops and eateries.

Inside a tenement building you can hear "Ping, ping…" sounds coming from one room. That's the manager's developmentally challenged daughter flinging poker chips into the bin by sorting out different colors. K, a man in his forties, walked by their doorway to the alcove on the third floor's back window by the fire escape to get some air. K is dressed in crumpled clothing because he washes them by hand since there is no washing machining in the tenement building and he sleeps in his clothes. While looking down the streets below the I-5 freeway, he saw a tank coming up the street and it came to a stop parallel to the building on Jackson Street and swung its large gun and aimed at the building. K is not surprised at all. He possessed the nuclear codes of China and this is not the first time they tried to intimidate him. After what seems like a minute of silence, K saw a police motorcycle came up the street and escort the tank further up the street.

K took a leak in the communal toilet and went back to his room #317 and called his mother and when his mother answered, this is what K and his mother said:

K: Mother, I stared them down again!

M: What you mean?

K: I saved the building!

M: What you mean?

K: I stopped them from killing 100 million flies.

M: You go to watch TV. I am cooking dinner.

K: With my X-ray vision, I see you are counting money

M: What you mean?

K: Always money, money, money, crazy and funny!

K's mother hung up on K. She didn't let him live in her Northgate split -level house. He lives on SSI and cooks on a hot-plate. He washes his clothes in a bucket with water from the water basin in the corner of the room. He was writing poetry and he keeps his rejected pile in a drawer. He suddenly feels lonely and so he removed the cardboard that acts as a blind to the window and stared down the streets below. He remembers suddenly that he forgot to take his medication so far today. He took his atypical antipsychotics and remembers that tomorrow he sees his nurse practitioner for more meds. He makes a telephone call to another mental patient.

He normally goes to the Denny Woo Park to sit on a bench for a while every day. It is sort of a ritual. But last week he saw a black man fornicating with a white prostitute there and so he stopped going to the park. He went back to writing a poem:

> Today I read Elizabeth
>
> She is double the NSA and the fire escape
>
> And Nanny Compoot Chuck Norris has this to say
>
> I won't fight Bruce Lee in the pink
>
> He is Li Po in drag
>
> If I knock him on his ass, all over the grass
>
> Half ding and half a ring
>
> I think I will read more of Elizabeth
>
> Doesn't Hitler too need a drink?

K is receiving "supportive therapy," because his case-manager thinks that his therapist from Hong Kong, Alice Chen, knows about his bicultural problems as a factor in his illness.

K suddenly feels depressed but he is afraid to go out the tenement doors yet because of the Chinese mafia that he fears. He has to wait until his cousin comes to see him. She is a Lee. She has connections.

She works in a garment shop, but K *knows* that she secretly owns it and not only that; she owns a chain of sweat shops stretching from San Francisco to Malaysia. Her father, his Uncle, is a member of the Triad. K sometimes has the feeling that Chinatown is encircled by two dragons: one black and one golden, mutually interlocked in a death combat. K's medication made him drowsy. He drank some hot cocoa and soon he was drifting off to sleep.

At the International Terrace:

It was near the end of the road for me. I was isolated in a high rise low-income apartment in Seattle Chinatown, being taken advantage of because of my isolation and mental illness. Threats seem to come from everywhere and nowhere. Even Chrysanthemum, by quite a coincidence was an old Japanese lady in her nineties living all alone in the next apartment on the eleventh floor with me, separating by cinder blocks. My literary zine was called Chrysanthemum that I was trying to resurrect. A couple of times mail came to me mistakenly delivered and knocked on the old lady's door to give it to her. She was very petite and delicate, as many Japanese women are with that exotic object-like feel. Oh, but they are not toys, as I found out with Eileen, my first girlfriend, who was my first pain. I was still thinking of that pain, which ended just months before. And it still lingered.

The tomblike feel of the high rise apartment, though spacious as far as real estate in Chinatowns goes, was never a home. If I drop a penny on the floor, it will sound like dropping a big kettle on the floor to the people below me. I didn't have money to buy a rug or to carpet the place and more than once, when I first moved in; the "brother" of the Japanese lady singer came up in the middle of the night to complain. I could not distinguish nights from days when I first moved in, no schedules, and nothing to do. I even played Go against myself until I felt I was a hopeless prisoner never to be exchanged.

Then Holly Smith, editor of the *International Examiner*, the neighborhood paper asked me to write an article on safety in Chinatown. I wrote the following article, which later was edited down and published in 1996. This article generated the most controversy in the history of the newspaper and Holly Smith was relieved of her position as editor.

To Achieve Greater Safety in the International District:

My Uncle Sum was a member of the Canton Police force in China for over 40 years. His one advice for law and order: "Live within your income, no matter what income that is." For most of his tenure, spanning three governments – the Nationalists, The Japanese Occupation, and the People's Republic of China, the police were not allowed to carry guns. They were required to document a case and wait two weeks before obtaining a gun from the bureau after a formal request. The policeman had to state precisely whom and why he was arresting.

As one can see, this kind of reservation on the use of force places a greater responsibility and risks on the policeman. My Uncle Sum just muses, "Doesn't a cat risk its life to catch a mouse?" The emphasis is on intelligence and planning, taking into account of all the social, sociological, and political forces at work, and to keep in mind that economics is the underlying factor that pervades everything.

As an I.D. dweller for over 10 years, waking up to mice in ecstasy in the middle of the night in the aptly-named Republic Hotel tenement, to talk myself back to sleep, and then only to have Lisa Poon, the woman across the hall in #316 rap on my door at 2 A.M. to read a document for her. It turns out to be a deed to a house that her boyfriend had won in a card game, and to make sure the loser did not give them something bogus.

Another time, there was a real emergency when Miao Ying knocked on my door in the middle of the night. Her 80-year-old father Rui Kuang wanted me to call a cab for them. They were too timid to ask me to help them. At my questioning, Mr. Kuang revealed that he could not urinate due to a prostate problem. Going out in the night with no English was like sailing toward the middle of the ocean with a leaky boat. So, I got dressed and called a cab and the cab left us off at the Pacific Medical Center clinic. The cab left before we discovered that the clinic was closed. Miao Ying and Rui would have been stuck there. Luckily there was a telephone booth and I called another cab to take us to the public hospital Harborview Medical Center on Yesler hill overlooking Chinatown. We waited a long time until Mr. Kuang's face was turning blue because we did not come by ambulance. Finally a nurse came and inserted a foley through Mr. Kuang's penis to the bladder to drain his urine.

The safety issue here at the I.D. is ultimately about money – whether someone breaks into your car, rob you at gun point, the offer of prostitution, or the sale of drugs is about money. Money, according to Uncle Sum, is the ability to do ten-thousand things, and yet it is the ten-thousand evils. Money, though everyone should have a certain amount of, but it is to despise its immoral acquisition or use that society can be just. And so, crime is a direct measure of the values of a given society.

The fact is, Seattle's International District (Chinatown) and all the Chinatowns in America are two-tiered societies. The businessmen and the affluent Chinese and other Asians are here in the day and in the evening be at their suburban homes counting their money made off the backs of recent immigrants, when the crimes take place in Chinatown. I have been unable to identify a single shop owner in Chinatown who in fact lives in Chinatown.

Who are "imprisoned" here are recent immigrants, the flop hotel dwellers, the disabled, the transients and the tortured souls. The business of trying to upgrade Chinatown means to remove these people who have to be here. In fact, the Republic Hotel several years ago decided to renovate when there was a grant from the city to do so. The owners and the PDA (a private housing authority) asked me to write a damaging article about the hotel in this newspaper. They offered me the manager's job for the renovated building or a staff writer's position with this newspaper. I went along until I figured out what they were doing.

I thought of the 95-year-old Vietnamese Chinese man who lives here and even though he has to climb the stairs to the third floor, he is in his waters because of the food, the gossip, the respect paid him. If he were to relocate to Ballard or some other neighborhood where he has to transfer on three busses to come back to Chinatown for his Pho and Chinese newspaper, he would feel lonely and like a fish out of the water, because no one is going to speak to him in Chinese or Vietnamese, "How's venerable grandpa today?" I started thinking the meaning of a community.

Safety also involves the perception of the community one lives in. The people who commute here to work such as the two-receptionists at the Wing Luke Asian Museum I talked with are Mary Jean and Yoshie. They have opposite feelings. The world traveler Mary Jean sees the I.D. as being very sedate even though the USA is the most dangerous place in the world to live in. Yoshie, meanwhile, a young woman from Tokyo, which is very safe and secure in her experience, was alarmed to hear that cars are stolen and people robbed in the parking lot under the freeway on Jackson and King Streets.

The residents here in the I.D. see a big improvement in recent weeks when the Seattle Police stepped up its patrols. I normally get up early and walk around Chinatown at 6 in the morning and see that prostitution at Hing Hay Park has stopped. However, around the first of the month, there are prostitutes that prowl across the street where I live, The International Terrace, a Seattle public housing site mainly for senior citizens. I live there because I am disabled. However, as a rule, I do not go out between 9 pm and 6 am, and most of the non-speakers of English do likewise.

When one talks to "Uncle Lau" and his compatriot Mr. Liu, whom everyone addresses differentially as "Ah Pak" for "Venerable Uncle," who together know just about everyone in Chinatown. They say that they do not venture out much after 7 pm. They don't do so because of the Vietnamese and Filipinos who hang around and ask for money. As far as these two older gentlemen know, these "beggars" aren't extorting the businesses and the restaurants, possibly because of the Chinese Culinary Union, which is a national syndicate. They are doing persistent panhandling, which creates a bad environment for food and entertainment.

A few years ago, there was a genuine social and legal pressure put upon the merchants who sold fortified wine:

("The Snow Man" ---- by Koon Woon as homage to Wallace Stevens).

"The Snow Man"

One must have a bottle of Gallo in this cold alley
And to shake the cops and other winos
And be on the lookout for some sucker to roll.

It has been a long time since my abode
Was taken from me not because of ice or lice
But because of the drive for condos

That in this high-rise reaching town,

Where all the Californ Dreaming has lost ground
To the sound of broken bottles,

Which is the brittle psyche of fife,
Which leads the rats from places bare
To places that no longer sustain life.

For the dweller of the alley, who is on dope,
And nothing, I mean nothing, beats a quick fix,
Nothing that is pure nor is impure.

The abuse of fortified wine led to aggressive panhandling, disorderly behavior, and public nuisance. But even when fortified wine sales ceased, merchants at the Gold Star Deli across from Hing Hay Park continued to sell beer and wine to transients in the park and those in nearby cheap hotels. Isn't this what America is all about though – to make a profit. Social ills? We can always resolve those later. This is good old Yankee optimism.

However, Ms. Jordan, probably a front for the Chinese shareholders of the Alps Hotel, is an enlightened entrepreneur. When the two-year lease of the Star Deli was up, Jordan gave the deli owner, a former waitress at the China Gate Restaurant for 15 years, the option to convert either into a noodle shop or a Taiwanese style teahouse. Or to forfeit the lease. The deli owner had several conversations with this writer, whose family has been in the restaurant business for generations, told her that there is a financial risk couple with more labor as a noodle house, but its location is excellent for it is smack dab in the heart of Chinatown. Fearing headaches, the deli owner sold and got out. This is another failure following the failure of a vegetarian restaurant kitty corner from it. Over time, the good restaurants have moved out to the suburbs with the advent of shopping malls and ample parking. Chinatown began to dwindle, and with less and less foot-traffic at night, it becomes more hazardous to maneuver in Chinatown.

Lao – Tzu, who is quoted only less than Jesus and he said that "ruling a large nation is like cooking a small fish." That is the crux of the problem. If there is too much police control and presence, this will "overcook" the fish. Whenever a force is imposed from the outside, it is a relegation of self-rule, autonomy and degenerates into heavy-handed policies. It is best left to the people who know themselves to govern themselves. There is always the expenses of a police presence and who ultimately pay for it is the taxpayers. And since Chinatown visitors who patronize restaurants and gift shops and so on are the ones end up paying a higher price for their purchases, they will stop coming to Chinatown, at which point the recent immigrants will lose their jobs or hours of work. Already there are vans transporting Chinatown laborers out to the suburbs to work at more affluent restaurants.

So now, as to the feeling of personal safety, something is reversing the tide of insecurity. It is wonderful to see practitioners of tai-chi and sword-play being coached by international famous masters at Hing Hay Park, as if people are reclaiming their public space. And you can hear the students of Gungfu led by grandmaster John S.S. Leung from the second floor of the martial arts store shouting rhythmically their moves. Yes, as to the crime problem in Chinatown, I say, "True, false, and unknown." True there is a crime problem in Chinatown; false that the real problems of economic inequity are being address, and unknown is whether people will make the necessary economic sacrifices to win back a community.

[Then I wrote that a copy of this editorial will be sent to the Canton Police in China for the Police Bureau Library].

Chinatown, Seattle

When the light is with you,
the dust is behind an old gift shop.
Faded memories are displayed in the window.
Persistent footsteps have descended down these curbs
for humbow retreats. Footfall killing time.

Frayed stairs of tenements bring down bitter strength.
Through alley doors furious wokking
below Chinatown family association halls.
Pigeon feathers and other disorders
flutter down these streets. Footfall killing time.

On Weller Street roast ducks are hung,
headless, dripping fat, next to
The Proprietress of Love, and three flights of stairs
lead up to a den of poverty. Unwashed windows face
out at tarry streets. Footfall killing time.

Construction workers face-lift the train station
and the sports dome is about to be imploded.
All the discussion at dim-sum before the tea kettle whistles.
Drainage pipes complain of rust and leakage
in these back streets. Footfall killing time.

On a spring day the sun mild and modest,
tender green foliage reappears on inner city street.
Or on a fall day at sundown warm and emberly
as the ferry traverses the sound,
the maples are three or four shades of yellow and brown
when lightly you walk upon these streets,
Footfall killing time.

Egg Tarts

Once talking to Maria, she's Greek, worried
About bi-cultural adaptation, asked me
If I like Chinese girl or American, told me
When she doesn't feel Greek, she'll buy baklava.

I squelch diary, querulous birds in hell &
Go to Ten Thousand Thigns Have Mothers Bakery
While Chinatown rust travels from building
To building, shop to shop.

It's a trick to feel Chinese even in Chinatown
Where tour buses inch along, the driver pointing out
Its exotic features while winos slump,
Street people, tattooed guns and knives,
Benevolent orders tight-lippedly banging
Mahjong, It'd take some articulate she-poet
To slit my bamboo frame: Opaque, hard, and abuse-
Resistant outside, but inside, a cavity,
Flip-flopping to dissonant winds, to needs.

Yellow lights of pagoda lanterns,
Unabashed verses, not wind through sparse bars,
Not winds through bamboo groves,
Papaya-ginger breath, I am not bamboo but arrows.
Now, Maria, I go for egg tarts to feel Chinese.

Little sweet buddhas behind beaded curtains
At 3 A.M., fashioned by Fushi, the god of creation,
Received by yellow bands and minds,
Belly-filling as verses translated from the Tang.

Grief:

Maybe under extreme stress or duress I could write about some parts of my life, which metamorphosize into a literary life and it was quite accidental.

[I nearly drowned three times in the village pond because it was grief from separation with my mother. I was about 4 when I "fell into" the village pond three times and grandmother burnt incense. The arguments I had with village women was anger toward my mother. Then leaving my grandmother. And China itself.]

I "killed" my grandmother in my mind almost two decades before she died. I caught the jet alone to leave China for America at age eleven. I had to leave her in China. I was her "little man" and I caught fish for her, watered her gardens, and gotten up at 3 AM to help her make pastries for the holidays. She was the source of news about my father. I don't remember her talking about my mother then. I could have suppressed all these memories. And what I remembered is selective and that is not the work of solely the conscious mind either.

I would be watching the older boys fishing off the pier into the village pond. I don't know how I was so clumsy that three times I had falling in and drank a belly full of water when an older boy lifted me out. It was all the more mysterious because the water was not over my head. I just lie face down in the water until I am groggy. Someone would send for my grandmother. That's when she would trot the fastest she could in her bound feet. Later she would burn incense to invoke the gods to protect me, but the gods must be hard of hearing, because it happened three times. I asked my psychiatrist if I was trying to commit suicide, unless I was unpopular for some reason and the other boys wanted to teach me a lesson. I was only four years old though and if there had been enemies, they would be my father and mother's.

Now, with my life nearing the end, I surmise it was some kind of attempt to seek help. I was grieving!

My father and mother had immigrated to America. I was left with my grandmother and an "adopted" sister at age two. So, my difficulties as a boy in China was anger toward my parents, especially toward my mother and that was why I engaged in quarrels with village women my mother's age. My grandmother hardly ever let me out of her sight but she would talk to me as we work together. She would tell me things about my father. She did not say as much about my mother I seem to not recall that.

My Auntie Siem said, "All one has to do is to take one look at you and know you are a communist boy!"
She waited for us in Shenzhen, which at that time was just a railway station on the Hong Kong side. On the Mainland side, it was some military barracks where they process legitimate immigration.

San Francisco Years:

"A Season in Hell"

"When you come in to work each morning,
remove your bodily organs and limbs
one by one. Hang them up on the hooks provided in
the walk-in box, then put a white apron
onto your disembodied self, pick up a knife,
and go to the meat block," said Alex the manager.

I was also drained of blood and other vital bodily fluids.

After the morning rush preparing pork adobo and chicken curry, I
ate lunch with Fong the chief cook and Lee the dishwasher.

In the afternoon, I examined souls and kept their merits and demerits in a ledger.

For the three months I worked at City Lunch near the Bart Station,
I paid my rent and gradually became robust enough to walk to work.
The entire city of San Francisco swung with the rhythm of my walk,

and stars appeared in the middle of the afternoon with a
sliver of the moon.

Meanwhile, at Fisherman's Wharf, the stingrays came to the
jetty
and whipped their tails against rocks; tourists paid me to
dance on
the waves. I carefully tread water and remembered to
breathe.

In the end, I was evicted anyway from my castle that glowed
at night.
For lack of anything better to do, I walked from hilltop to
hilltop,
burned newspapers to inhale the smoke, then climbed down
to the water
beneath the Golden Gate Bridge and harvested seaweed.

I waited until one sunny day when the water was warm and
calm,
then swam all the way to Asia and got replacements for my
disembodied self.
I did not forget that I was a ghost. And
that was my first season in Hell.

Vignette:

Can't afford anything this night but the streets, walking by Foster's I see a man prone and motionless on the sidewalk. I go next door to alert the hotel clerk that possibly someone is dead. He hurries out. Upon shaking the man by his ankles, the clerk has this to say, "Don't worry about him; he is just in a drunken stupor." I then keep on walking on Market Street. San Francisco at night is neon. I still have not claimed my baggage at the Greyhound Depot. I need to find Fred and Alex. They are a gay couple I knew in Seattle. But now it is three in the morning. I impulsively come down to San Francisco, and although I have relatives here, I don't feel like I can meet them like this. I need to walk some more hours until it is dawn in North Beach. I have only a twenty bill in my wallet, a choice between breaking it on a pack of Marlboro or a cup of coffee and a donut at Foster's. I could not make decisions like these and that is the reason they reject me from the Army. Sally says that I have to measure a sandwich with a ruler before I cut it in half.

The Stockton Hotel:

Earlier in Seattle, when I arrived, when I was 19, I hung around The Last Exit on Brooklyn, a coffeehouse in the University District. Neighbors from Aberdeen showed me the place and I fancied myself an intellectual to be. We were introduced to hash shish and Herman Hess. Ya, the Bead Game! Then some of my friends suggested I take a trip to San Francisco.

I drove down the coastal 101 with this little queer and pervert Jason Victor, except I didn't know that at the time.

He told me he was a photographer with his oversized Nikon with a zoom lens, like it was an oversized dick for him. I vaguely heard rumors that he had been thrown off the Fremont Bridge three times in Seattle.

[You should check out where they live, what friends and neighbors they have, and how do they get their income, etc.]

We were just sitting around in the Last Exit, a coffeehouse made famous or infamous by these misfits of society as well as some of its geniuses. For example, the chess champs of Washington State played chess here, including John Braille, who never wears socks or shoes, not even in winter, but he had a car and so it was not like he was imitating Jesus or anything. Some of my "friends" suggested that I take a trip to San Francisco with Jason Victor. I thought it was a good idea too at the time, since I have relatives there, and also so was my next door neighbor from Aberdeen. So, I got their address by letter, and drove down with Jason Victor, little knowing that it was a scheme cooked up to separate Eileen and me. She and I were dating and things were going rather slowly, and in my impatience, I thought a little time off from each other would be good. There were all kinds of signs that it would not work, then or ever, but my "best" friends suggested that I ought to see San Francisco for their own ends, and anyway, that was 1969, and all the flower children were heading that way. And Eileen was a very winsome looking Japanese-American.

[You should look at what is their motivation, what things of yours they may want, what skills you have that they might exploit, and what connections you have that may be of use to them.]

So, we were at the Stockton. Soon enough Crazy Annie was yelling at people on the street from her second floor window when we exit the backdoor. Patrick and William E. would give me marijuana or THC but I never took anything else. Patrick and William E. were a gay couple and I knew them in Seattle, and of course, Patrick was my next door neighbor in Aberdeen and he was my first contact in Seattle and when I first drove up to Seattle, they lived in a Hippie commune in Wallingford. Only John was working and he worked for Boeing. He rented the whole house. I was puzzled out of my gourd as to the social structure of this commune. Hayseed beat his girl friend and she was always bare from the waist up, with gorgeous tits and she also had a pretty face. Hayseed fancied himself a poet and read his poetry on Wednesday open-mics at the Last Exit. There was a woman named Susan but I can't say for sure. Then there were Patrick and William E. who introduced me to the Last Exit and to the greasy spoon on the upper Ave called the Hasty Tasty. I would end up spending my crucible years at these two places and a couple of years later, when I could drink legally, would also go across the street from the Hasty Tasty to the Century Tavern or go to the Blue Moon, my less favorite.

[Who do they want to be seen with? What do they not to be seen with?]

As I recall these fragments now in 2015, what, four and a half decades later, I can see why I didn't succeed in much of anything, and I can see it clearly now. The problem was that I thought Judy Collins wrote the song "Clouds" when it was Joni Mitchell who wrote and sang "Both Sides Now." I always got it second-hand. She really had been a coffeehouse singer who gave up a love child.

[What don't they tell you? Why is there subjects they avoid? Are there any unexplained gaps in their lives?]

But there was a Good Samaritan. Dr. Jacobs. We called him Larry, a psychiatrist on the UW faculty. He came in with a book by R.D. Laing called The Politics of Experience and he talked about Fritz Pearls' Gestalt Therapy. Hey, I thought, that is very interesting stuff, but it really hadn't pertained to me yet. Now if you were to write about all the successes and mishaps of just the Last Exit itself, you would discover enough materials here to fill an entire textbook of Abnormal Psychology. Dr. Jacobs will come in and out of this story and so we will let things develop of their own accord.

[So, set the story properly from the beginning. There will be good guys and bad guys but they are all human, though some are pettier than others.]

Patrick and William E. would take me hitch-hiking to Big Sur to go camping. After we set up tent, it would be nightfall as we cooked with our hobo stove over a campfire. All I could think of is food. And we would sleep together in the tent with me being in the middle. We were fully-clothed and in the morning, I wandered off to the beach after breakfast, after declining to take acid with the two. Later on, I would fail to find the two of them as I climbed onto a big boulder and sat and read Kafka's The Castle. It was incomprehensible, similar to the philosophy lectures of Professor John Wisdom which would come two years later.

Back at the Stockton when we come back from camping, we found out a couple of people had been knifed to death over drug deals. But on the second floor, which is where all the Chinese older people lived, Caucasians are seldom permitted to live there. We lived on the third floor. There I met Ruth and her one armed boyfriend, who was said to have a scholarship to college for writing. Four years later I met Ruth at the Tutorial Center for EOP at the UW, and all this time Ruth remembered my name. I did meet with her although I was on a Hegel and Marx kick at that time. A black lady Pat was the coordinator at the EOP.

The first Sky River Folk Rock Festival I attended. An aftermath of which is seeing "castles in the sky" when I drove the postal truck. I honestly believe most irrationally that there was such a life.

My father used to come to my room and shout at me. To this day, I don't know the reason for it. I wanted to be a chess bum and a street musician and wanted to get out!

In China, what they tell me. My uncle Chay would let me smoke the water pipe after placing a paper Yuan bill on the ground and bid me to take three puffs of the water pipe with lit tobacco and tells me that if I could pick it up, it would be mine. He would also spin me around three times, but I was so disoriented I couldn't even see straight. The ground was spinning and I could not pick up the Yuan bill and I finally fell over. They laughed. That's why I never thought seriously of Chay. I am just going to put these facts out there and I don't care where the chips may fall.

It is old Hom the manager. His retarded daughter and his schizophrenic wife.

An undiscovered ghost:

Like a ghost I walked up and down the Ave in the middle of the night after the Exit and the Coffee Corral and the Hasty Tasty looking in window displays of mannequins. The time I needed money to extract a tooth, the morning after the Wah Mee Massacre.

[I live outside of it all, or on the periphery. I was the Canton policeman who kept an eye on the Honey Court Restaurant because they gave me hot tea when I first became homeless in Seattle Chinatown. Before that, homeless after John moved out of the Pine Street apartment after being kicked out of Fat Aunt's place.]

[There is no beginning, no middle, and no ending.
Everything just got thrown into place.
The Doors - into this world we are thrown. There is no music, just pragmatism.]
"You are always doing things that don't need to be done!"

It very an unhealthy environment.. My father comes to my room and screams at me, "You have no responsibility!" I don't know what I did wrong. At most, it was something that I didn't' do. When I first came over from China, he started grooming me by making me make his cup of mud coffee, while he watches football on television, with the siblings chimping over the sofa.
And I have to learn to serve him. Breaking me in.

Chongwai (bed space)

"Hey, you keep your army of cockroaches on your side of the chongwai!"

The Chongwai was only bunk bed space that was our private space that we slept and ate on. There was no privacy. Although we had access to the communal areas (the bathroom with a tub and the communal kitchen), for anything else, we had to restrict ourselves on our chongwai. The more "prosperous" tenants on the flat had tiny rooms but at least they can fornicate quietly.

Looking back, that was really a mean thing to say to the old woman, without anyone to care for her, and possibly mentally ill. Maybe all she could have done was to keep herself alive, and then what about after that?

I used the bunk bed for a desk as I sat in a small square stool for my homework. I was already twelve and I slept with my grandmother.

I iron my clothes and shined my shoes and scrubbed my own clothes. We hung them to dry on a bamboo pole from the front of the flat above the street.

The woman above gave me magazines to read and one was about an affair.

All the women were trying to capture a gimwhanhak (A Chinese bachelor in the US).

Homeless

Gene and I mainly went to the Goodwill. Because it was a good walk and because the Goodwill on Rainier had a café in the back that was cheap and we could sit out in the garden, we liked to spend time there. There was absolutely nothing for me to do except to wait. It was like an arrogant butcher saying, as arrogant as a mathematician, "If it takes twenty years to injure, it takes twenty years to heal." My mind was blank and the world looked vacant to me. I was furthermore on heavy meds and I lack the ability to feel any pleasure, the clinical word for it was "anhedonia."

Gene was my "companion" and I bought him food. He was working and homeless, sleeping at the shelter with me. Gene was an MBA one time and his wife divorced him, and he became depressed and talked to a psychiatrist, and the more and more he talked about wanting to get a gun and shoot himself in the head, the more real it seemed. Rather than to do that, he joined the Peace Corp and went to Africa. He was disappointed he said because his Midwest wheat growing knowledge as a farm boy was useless, because the Africans were not interested in growing wheat. He really identified with the song "Amazing Grace." He took on so much self-blame, but he was very selfish or self-center as the only reason he hang around me was because I received SSI and had cash. He was saving his money to go back to Minnesota or Wisconsin was he was from. It was also a bit better for me to have someone around even though I was so exhausted all the time. He was a night clerk at the Atlas. But they would not let me rent there. There was a tenant there by the month let me say his name is Jim. Jim was undereducated and I suspect had some kind of legal problem in the past, but he was the only guy that helped me to store my one suitcase that held my citizenship paper. Jim showed me the crossword puzzles he was doing to increase his vocabulary. He was very proud of learning new words. He is never seen in Chinatown streets. He goes to work early and comes back and no one knows where he works. He was from the South.

Cityscape with Solitary Figure

Not a sparrow is yet up, nor the milk trucks.
Even to malign him, the street lamps are frugal.
He who is under the shadow of the building, a deeper shadow.
He who hauls his house on his back.
Must we avoid acknowledging him?
He whose going does not make an arriving.

In the darkness he is white, brown, or black -
No one can tell or would tell.
He knows the various grids of the city and how far
Into the morning before he can get a free cup of coffee.
The park benches are partitioned
And signs saying no camping. What a life!

Formerly there was shelter from the rain
Beneath the bridge, but the stench of graffiti
Forced him to brightly-lit doorways before dawn.
Merchant-hired security sweeps him
Up in the morning and he goes as a lump
Of coal in the snow, going just for the sake of go.

I always have felt small and insignificant except when I have my grandiose moments gratis of my illness, and then, my grandiosity is so great that I believe it is easily the greatest delusion in the history of mankind. One time I reduced all philosophic logic to three parameters: True, False, and Unknown, and when used as verifiers, these three logical values can resolve *any* philosophical problem. So, take a moment from your preoccupations and join me from a perspective in Wonderland. America is close to that point already, ready to manufacture *realities* in many possible worlds. But for now, I want to return to my Uncle Sum's village for it is still somehow enchanted though lost to time. Therefore, the past is solipsistic and takes a mind to recreate and behold it. Enough nonsense, let the backward journey begin as in Edward Bellamy's Looking Backward.

I lived with Uncle Sum's mother. She is my maternal grandmother. She was from the Liu Village who married into the Lee Village. But now with both my parents overseas in America, she came to my village to take care of me when I was just two. I called her "Ah Po," meaning "dear grandma." But sometimes I call her "dragon ears" in Chinese because she was hard of hearing. I was an extremely difficult child. Too much nervous energy and too devilish.

I loved the water. And there is the village pond, our own for our village was as large as the village itself. We raise fish in it, we wash our clothes there, and the boys swim in it. I caught small trout and loaches for my grandmother, although I didn't like to eat small fish.

"Ruling a large nation is like cooking a small fish." --- The Tao Te Ching.

One of our neighbors had the best dirt beneath the bricks in front of their house laid for a walkway. The old man was possibly mentally ill, his nickname was Opium K. We kids shuck corn to give him the corn silk for "tobacco" and he gladly accepted it. His daughter-in-law took care of him and she had two young children, both too young to fish in the village pond. The woman asked me to give her son a fish or two, as I used their worms. I was an honest merchant. I started out honest ☺. And so I gave them 1/3 of my catch. Grandmother was always overjoyed when I bring fish home. Those small fish were almost microscopic but I think my grandmother was thrilled that I loved her.

The eye of the needle

She said you can see the world through
The eye of the needle,
Writing as she with her index finger
On my spine.
She said the whorl on your
Back indicates

You have great strength,
Like an ox,
And she patiently plucked
Hair from my forehead,
Saying,
This will make you generous.

Grandmother your aged hands were
Soft.
If I only knew the number
Of Chickens
You have plucked
Gently naked,
Undressing them for the next life.

And you rubbed
Your grandchildren's foreheads
To gentle sleep with those
Palms.
Tender tendrils of garden petals
You rubbed between finger tips
Loved they were and abounded

I forgive the time you hacked
To pieces my dog and scooped it
Steaming onto my plate.
I didn't have enough meat.

Grandmother
You are not here now
And I am strong
You wrote a whorl on my back.

"The humble is the root of the noble.
The low is the foundation of the high."

Uncle Sum Again

My Uncle Sum was among the poorest of the poor in his village. I love him because his location in the village was as deep as his thoughts. His house was on the corner of the village that through a bamboo thatch it led to a small pine forest. And in the bamboo thatch were wine that his family produced wine in old days, and they had the reputation of their whiskey for healing bruises often associated with the practice of Gungfu.

Eventually, walking past rice paddies, little streams, and this windowless house people were hushed about, and more villages I arrived at the bamboo thatch that was the entrance to my Uncle's village. It was called Bow Lung, some 8 *lis* from my village, or approximately 2 2/3 miles.

Bow Lung village was my mother's side of the family. I had two uncles there. There was a third one but he immigrated to Peru. I always go first to my Uncle Sum's house.

My image of it was that it was quiet and orderly, even though he had a wife and four children. I remembered him dusting the furniture with a feather duster. I also knew that if a child misbehaves, he gets whacked by the handle of the feather duster on the palm of the hand, with the teacher holding the feather part of the punishing instrument. In my entire life I was only whacked once in a private school in Hong Kong when I was in the fourth grade, for not completing my homework on time.

My aunt would slaughter a chicken if they had one on such an occasion. And I would always get a drumstick. My Uncle would take down the abacus from the shelf. The abacus is a tray of beads that slides up or down in many columns to represent numbers. My Uncle told me that each configuration of the abacus represents a state of the universe. He told me that by learning the numerical chants that go with flicking the beads up or down, I could calculate faster with my fingers than with my brain.

Across the years I've lost the chants. But I'd sit quietly and observe his fingers add, subtract, multiply and divide, like grains harvested and divided among the villagers, like women begetting children and they in turn multiply, and divide again all their wealth among all their generations to come.

All this took place in their simple house, in front of the bamboo thicket that hid the family's ancient wine vat, where cherries and plums had dipped in various ages, in time of Tartars and Missionaries.

My Uncle said, after each transaction, you must restore the instrument to the zero or empty position, for nothing is ever gained or lost in any transaction, it is always equals paired with equals, finally 0 = 0, then you have peace.

Let's backtrack a little bit on the story. In the West, the future King pulls a sword with its blade embedded in a rock, while all others who try to do so fails. In China, the person of authority in some quarters of society is a member of the Triad, and his symbol of power is the abacus. China has three religions (Buddhism, Confucianism, and Taoism). A member of the Triad is sworn to be a protector of all three.

I was told by my mother, as soon as I was able to understand, but never to know the truth or falsity of which, that upon my first birthday, as it was customary for being a first born son, be placed on the ground with an array of objects in front of me. All the male elders would attend this ceremony. My head was shaven and I crawled toward the various objects placed in front of me. These would include a comb, candy, ink and brush, a piece of cloth, a musical instrument, a book, and assorted toys, and an abacus. The first object that I would pick up was to determine my fate and future occupation.

I picked up the abacus, a *hsuen pan*, meaning variously as "a calculating device," "a tray of vinegar," or "a vat of sorrow." Whereas in the West, the staff is the symbol of power, in some recesses of China, the abacus denotes authority.

My Uncle Sum taught me to do calculations on the abacus when I was five years old. He taught me to chant while flipping the wooden beads up and down the wooden tray. The chants enabled me to do the calculations without thinking of the mathematics itself. It is like an algorithm that can be performed by anyone, regardless of one's mathematical ability or insights. I was merely a robot, operating the world's first computer, which now is proven to be mathematically equivalent to a Turing Machine, which is the theoretical computer that all electronic computers are models of. Uncle Sum was my tutor, the equivalent of a godfather in the West.

Uncle Sum, my second maternal uncle, had inherited the family business when he was 19 years old, the year he got married to his first wife. He had an older brother, my Uncle Jose who had immigrated to Peru to join his second-maternal uncle there, when he was just twelve.

The family business was a small brewery. They made whiskey for medicinal use. The main use was for blood circulation, which got rid of bruises and strengthened the body generally speaking. Uncle Sum's father, or my late grandfather, had been an immigrant to Canada but I never saw him alive. My mother told me that he had died of dysentery along with a sister and a brother of hers when she was young. My maternal grandmother had lost three people in her family in one year.

My Uncle Sum then also took over the grocery store that they had in town. Something very sad happened. Uncle Sum's mother-in-law connived to get Uncle Sum's money. And remember he was just a young man at 19. The mother-in-law hired some professional gambler to entice Uncle Sum in gambling games and took all his money. That was the same year that his first wife died of syphilis. Apparently she had been unfaithful. People thought and accused Uncle Sum of having syphilis too but he never did. He lived to be 86 and died just last year in 2004 with a clear mind. Those were the lawless years during the Sino-Japanese War.

Later Uncle Sum went to Hong Kong and became a "merchant." What he dealt in we never were told, except that he got in with the wrong kind of people. He was beaten up and his face was cut deeply with a knife. He still had the half-moon scar the day he died. He had to spend several months recuperating in our Canton flat. After he recovered, he went back to the village and took another wife. He became a farmer, doing honest labor.

When the Communists took power in China in 1949, they asked Uncle Sum to be the village mayor. He refused. They asked him why not, since he is the most qualified person. He said, "I have many relatives and some of them might get into trouble with the government."

"So what?" The Communists said, "We are in charge now."

"The thing to consider is," said Uncle Sum, "I don't know how long your government would last, but my relatives last forever."

I remember going to the rice paddies outside of Uncle Sum's village Bow Lung with Uncle and my cousins to catch small crabs that come back from the river to procreate. They were called *pung kai.* They were so small they were practically just a shell. In fact they were so small that when they pinch you it didn't hurt much. We would gather them from the small streams alongside the rice paddies walking up stream so that we wouldn't stir up the mud and cloud up the water in front of us. Uncle Sum then would grind them up and ferment them. Nobody else in the village wanted them. Uncle was very frugal. I guess the *pung kai* sauce would taste all right if a person got used to them, like really fishy seafood or strong cheese. But I never got used to them. And so my second-aunt would always give me a chicken thigh, and the other one goes to her youngest son. I am Uncle Sum's godson. Chinese society is avuncular. Uncles have a lot of responsibility to nephews and nieces. In ancient China, I am told, if a nephew dies somewhere, he cannot be buried until one of his uncles has examined the body.

My village was named Nan On, or South Peace. Everyone is my village is named Lock. There are two other villages of the Lock clan adjacent to us. We are in the District of Sui Po in Toishan County, Kwangtung Province, on the southern coast of China. Back in the latter part of the 1800's, there was a great famine in Toishan. Most of the men immigrated to America as "indentured servants." My great-grandfather came to Hoquiam, Washington where he operated a laundry and had shares in a restaurant. He was called Lock Lick, meaning he was a Lock and he had great strength. His English ability was quite good and so the mayor of Hoquiam went with him to the Lock villages to conscript 500 men to come over to build rails to logging areas. Old rail tracks can still be found in the woods in places like Humptulips, Washington. People also say that every once in a while, they would find a discarded opium bottle. One of these men that my great-grandfather brought over was no other than the grandfather of our former governor Gary Locke (his family had anglicized their name). Well, then, why is my name Woon then? And not Lock?

Because of US immigration policy for much of Chinese American history, Chinese women were not allowed to come with their men. So Chinese immigrants went back to China for conjugal visits. Every time they go back to China, they'd report that they sired a son. And there will be a paper "documenting" that claim. My grandfather was supposedly an opium addict who lived a wasted life and died somewhere in Canada, where and how no one seems to know. He never reported that he had a son in China, his son being my father. And so when my father immigrated to the US, he purchased a "paper son" immigration paper from the Woon family and came over to the US as a Woon. He was interrogated at Angel Island where Chinese immigrants were quarantined. My father thus assumed a false identity. And thus I am known as Koon Woon, when most Chinese people know that I am a Lock.

Again, according to my mother, and what she tells me that I don't know the truth or falsity of which, my father was a gifted painter when he was just sixteen. He had sold some of his paintings when he was in normal school. The teachers were going to send him to Nanking, the southern capital of China at that time, to the National Academy to study art. His mother didn't allow him to go. One day, she hired a bicycle messenger to go to my father's boarding school. The message was, "Go home to your mother, she's dying." He hurried home in the middle of classes. But when he got home, she was perfectly all right. He asked why she had called him home. She told him that she wanted him to get married and have a son before she dies. She wanted to see a grandson.

The villagers got busy when they had heard that my father was an eligible marriage partner. A suitable match was made. My mother, then a young maiden of sixteen, was brought over to my father's house and they were seated far apart. They had a glimpse of each other but no words were spoken between the two of them.

My paternal grandmother said to my maternal grandmother that the girl looked all right. She told my maternal grandmother that she wanted so many moon cakes and so many rolls of cloth as dowry and that my maternal grandmother was not to show her daughter to anyone else. Thus my mother and father were married when they were both sixteen. And as it was customary, my mother came to live in my father's house. But it would be ten years before I would be born. And when I would be two years old, my mother would leave me to join my father in America and leave me to the care of my maternal grandmother until I was nearly twelve, when I would board a jet all alone and fly to Sea-Tac Airport. That's when I would see my parents again and to see six siblings all born in the US.

This is getting ahead of the story. When my father immigrated to America he joined his sister, my Fat Aunt Lock Gim Gee, in San Francisco. He worked in the Oakland Shipyards as a torch cutter on naval ships. He also went to night school to learn English. He was making good money, like many people in World War II. But wastrels enticed him to gamble. He would have a lunch all made up in his lunch box on the way to work and these gamblers would ask him to go gambling. Since, Chinatowns were bachelor societies gambling was a good substitute for sex. He would lose all his money. He later told me that he had even slept on the streets. Finally, an older Chinese man asked him to go to Hollywood with him and work as a waiter. This he did. "I made enough money in wages and tips in one year that I was able to go back to China and see your mother," he later told me. Apparently for several years he had sent no money to my mother. He must have gone back in 1948 for I was conceived and born February 2, 1949. My mother came to America when I was two, leaving me to the care of my maternal grandmother and an adopted sister who is nine years older than I am.

I must have been a hyperactive kid. I fell into the village ponds three times. I'd been watching the older boys fishing and suddenly the next thing I remembered was that my maternal grandmother was there at the edge of the pond burning incense and offering prayers. Finally, she decided she couldn't watch over me all the time she went and begged the teachers to let me come to school a year early. And so I did start school a year early, but I was still hyperactive and I vaguely remember never being in my own seat, always bothering other students. And so I had to repeat the first grade.

But even before I attended school, I learned how to play poker. I was so good at it that I became the village card shark. I won all the marbles, matches, and picture cards from all the players in the village. When they ran out of tokens to play with me, I would lend it back to them. Then I would win it all back again. And so at school I played cards too during recess and lunch breaks. And eventually I won everything from everybody. Finally the teachers confiscated my deck of cards. I played hooky for two weeks. I would go roaming outside the village or go fishing during the time I would normally be in school. Of course my adopted sister knew about it, since I didn't follow her to school in the morning, she knew but she kept it a secret from my grandmother. Finally the teachers passed word along that if I were to go back to school; they would give me back my deck of cards. By this time, I missed my friends at school and so I went back.

We also had a "math-bee," sort of like "spelling bees" over here. In our math class, all the students were placed together in one large schoolroom. We would choose two sides to have a math contest. I was always the first one chosen. A student from each team would go up to the blackboard and do math problems. I usually face down many competitors and as always, our team would win.

And so to get ahead of the story a little bit, when I was in a private school in Hong Kong, a school examiner had come to our fourth grade math class. The teacher, a thin and sharp lady, asked me to go up to the board to do difficult problems. But I had been sick and missed a few days of school. I couldn't do the problem. My teacher was very angry with me. "Just because you been sick for a few days, you can't do any math?" She was embarrassed by me. Her reputation was tarnished. For she had probably picked a very difficult problem for me to do. It was a problem involving mixed fractions or something like that. A couple of students admonished me; "The Examiner took down your name. You will never be admitted to the University of Hong Kong." I don't know if that was really true. They got their revenge on me, who was the best math student in the class of every math class I was in so far.

Every year in May in our semi-tropical zone there are the monsoons. There will be an outburst of lightning and thunder and torrents of rain would fall. It would not quit for one day or two days, but it would rain for a couple of weeks until rain and water is everywhere. The roads will be covered with water. So would be the rivers and ponds and the outhouses would also be flooded and covered. Water would come inside the house. People would put their pigs up in the attic and their chickens shut in their coops. But it was warm rain. I would be inside hearing its incessant drone, feeling quite bored, but in a way, meditative, as meditative as a young boy could be.

It was dangerous to wade in the water. I could fall into a well or into the river or even into the village pond. And so I am restricted to home. Even the village yards are flooded and it is quite possible to catch a fish with a net anywhere.

Eventually, the water would recede. We are thankful for the water, for it would loosen and soften the mud in the rice paddies. Plowing begins as soon as the water recedes.

One event every post-monsoon time I like is going to the rice paddies with a bucket with my adopted sister. The sun would be out in early June after the water receded from the rice paddies. But some of the water is trapped inside the rice paddies because the paddies had small dikes. Rice plants require water to grow.

As the water gets warm, the fish that were trapped in the rice paddies would start to swim sluggishly near the surface of the water. We would simply pick them up. Also, the catfish would have burrowed themselves in holes they have dug with their heads into the dikes' banks. We would carefully reach in there and grab them, but once in a while their stickers gore us. My adopted sister and I fill our bucket with fish and that's the most fish we ever get for a year.

We come home quite happily of course. We would de-gut the fish and salt them and strung them on a pole to dry out in the sun. This we would steam in the winter. Sometimes someone in the village would steal one or two fish from our lot. My adopted sister would say to my grandmother that someone had stolen a fish or two. My grandmother's reply would be, "No, Ah Deel, the cat got them." My grandmother was very generous.

My grandmother, I am talking about my maternal grandmother now. My father's mother died before I was born.

My grandmother's feet were bound. They looked like two clumps of gingerroots. That, however, means that she came from a well-off family in pre-Mao China. She wasn't the peasant class. She wasn't supposed to work in the paddies. But with the Sino-Japanese war and their declining fortune, she eventually had to work in the fields, after bearing six children, four of which surviving childhood. Did my grandmother ever complain? No, she was stoic like a proper Buddhist that she was. Her only fault is cooking with wine with everything. I didn't particularly like the wine taste in my food. She would send me to the wine shop with an empty bottle in Canton when we lived there after we left the village. No one would raise an eyebrow to sell wine to a little boy. There just wasn't public drunkenness in Canton or anywhere I remember in China. My uncles and my grandmother gave me wine though. Sometimes for fun, they make me wear my grandmother's eyeglasses after I had three or four teacups of plum wine and ask me to walk a few steps. Then suddenly the floor moves up and down and I hear hissing in my ears, and I would hear my uncles laugh. They came from a family with a brewery, I remember, and so drinking is part of their lives.

When I was five, I would bend over in the rice paddies several paces behind the adults, plant rice seedlings one by one into the mud. When not planting rice seedlings, I would water grandmother's green gardens every morning and evening with a spout that I dip into the village pond. I watered the winter melon, the bokchoy, the cabbage, the pea plants, the corn, a few other varieties we grow rotationally, and then my two papaya trees that I grew.

I grew them from seeds when I was five. By the time I left the village when I was nine, I was able to harvest sweet papaya fruits.

On my ninth birthday in my village, I felt that there was something in the air. Many relatives came early to our house to do food preparation. This time, men, as opposed to women did the cooking. A long table was set up in the utility room of the house. We ate in three shifts. First the men, next the mature women, and finally the old women and young children. My Uncle Sum came to our house and that was the only time that I remember his coming over. He asked me to eat with the men. I felt so proud. I felt like a little man.

Where we were, so to speak:

We are the Lock clan. We are in the District of Sui Po in Toishan County, Kwangtung Province, on the southern coast of China. Back in the latter part of the 1800's, there was a great famine in Toishan. Most of the men immigrated to America as "indentured servants." My great-grandfather came to Hoquiam, Washington where he operated a laundry and had shares in a restaurant. He was called Lock Lick, meaning he was a Lock and he had great strength. His English ability was quite good and so the mayor of Hoquiam went with him to the Lock villages to conscript 500 men to come over to build rails to logging areas. Old rail tracks can still be found in the woods in places like Humptulips, Washington. People also say that every once in a while, they would find a discarded opium bottle. One of these men that my great-grandfather brought over was no other than the grandfather of our former governor Gary Locke (his family had anglicized their name). Well, then, why is my name Woon then? And not Lock?

Because of US immigration policy for much of Chinese American history, Chinese women were not allowed to come with their men. So Chinese immigrants went back to China for conjugal visits. Every time they go back to China, they'd report that they sired a son. And there will be a paper "documenting" that claim. My grandfather was supposedly an opium addict who lived a wasted life and died somewhere in Canada, where and how no one seems to know. He never reported that he had a son in China, his son being my father. And so when my father immigrated to the US, he purchased a "paper son" immigration paper from the Woon family and came over to the US as a Woon. He was interrogated at Angel Island where Chinese immigrants were quarantined. My father thus assumed a false identity. And thus I am known as Koon Woon, when most Chinese people know that I am a Lock.

And so to get ahead of the story a little bit, when I was in a private school in Hong Kong, a school examiner had come to our fourth grade math class. The teacher, a thin and sharp lady, asked me to go up to the board to do difficult problems. But I had been sick and missed a few days of school. I couldn't do the problem. My teacher was very angry with me. "Just because you been sick for a few days, you can't do any math?" She was embarrassed by me. Her reputation was tarnished. For she had probably picked a very difficult problem for me to do. It was a problem involving mixed fractions or something like that. A couple of students admonished me; "The Examiner took down your name. You will never be admitted to the University of Hong Kong." I don't know if that was really true. They got their revenge on me, who was the best math student in the class of every math class I was in so far.

Every year in May in our semi-tropical zone there are the monsoons. There will be an outburst of lightning and thunder and torrents of rain would fall. It would not quit for one day or two days, but it would rain for a couple of weeks until rain and water is everywhere. The roads will be covered with water. So would be the rivers and ponds and the outhouses would also be flooded and covered. Water would come inside the house. People would put their pigs up in the attic and their chickens shut in their coops. But it was warm rain. I would be inside hearing its incessant drone, feeling quite bored, but in a way, meditative, as meditative as a young boy could be.

It was dangerous to wade in the water. I could fall into a well or into the river or even into the village pond. And so I am restricted to home. Even the village yards are flooded and it is quite possible to catch a fish with a net anywhere.

Eventually, the water would recede. We are thankful for the water, for it would loosen and soften the mud in the rice paddies. Plowing begins as soon as the water recedes.

My grandmother's feet were bound. They looked like two clumps of gingerroots. That, however, means that she came from a well-off family in pre-Mao China. She wasn't the peasant class. She wasn't supposed to work in the paddies. But with the Sino-Japanese war and their declining fortune, she eventually had to work in the fields, after bearing six children, four of which surviving childhood. Did my grandmother ever complain? No, she was stoic like a proper Buddhist that she was. Her only fault is cooking with wine with everything. I didn't particularly like the wine taste in my food. She would send me to the wine shop with an empty bottle in Canton when we lived there after we left the village. No one would raise an eyebrow to sell wine to a little boy. There just wasn't public drunkenness in Canton or anywhere I remember in China. My uncles and my grandmother gave me wine though. Sometimes for fun, they make me wear my grandmother's eyeglasses after I had three or four teacups of plum wine and ask me to walk a few steps. Then suddenly the floor moves up and down and I hear hissing in my ears, and I would hear my uncles laugh. They came from a family with a brewery, I remember, and so drinking is part of their lives.

When I was five, I would bend over in the rice paddies several paces behind the adults, plant rice seedlings one by one into the mud. When not planting rice seedlings, I would water grandmother's green gardens every morning and evening with a spout that I dip into the village pond. I watered the winter melon, the bokchoy, the cabbage, the pea plants, the corn, a few other varieties we grow rotationally, and then my two papaya trees that I grew.

I grew them from seeds when I was five. By the time I left the village when I was nine, I was able to harvest sweet papaya fruits.

On my ninth birthday in my village, I felt that there was something in the air. Many relatives came early to our house to do food preparation. This time, men, as opposed to women did the cooking. A long table was set up in the utility room of the house. We ate in three shifts. First the men, next the mature women, and finally the old women and young children. My Uncle Sum came to our house and that was the only time that I remember his coming over. He asked me to eat with the men. I felt so proud. I felt like a little man.

I Have not Come to Kill My Father:

I have not come to kill my father. I have come to praise him.

Like a war orphan, I feel the strangeness of a *distant* father. He took my mother and her teats from me when I was two. Suddenly the hands that caressed me were wrinkled and chapped and old. They were my grandmother's hands that my mother gave me to. Gradually I had grown used to burlap instead of silk. The constancy of my grandmother was the Great Wall of China, the mulberry, the silkworms, the luxuriant bamboo forests, and the cicadas that sing only once in seventeen years. So I remained in the womb of China, never to be able to grow to the age of China itself, but always approaching it. So, my friend, you see my loss when I had to leave my grandmother and homeland when I was 11 to come to America to rejoin an already-made family – a family of Chinese tears and blood, which I thought had to be the best in the world, but in actuality, as I was to find out later, it was a pocket of servility. Like a war orphan, I was in America to ease the conscience of the Americans, and to contribute to their mastery of other peoples. But strong as they are, maybe there's a *chink* in their armor?

I now think of my father the first 10 years in America, his wife back in China, and so naturally he followed the hoodlums of San Francisco around, being the volley ball captain of SF Chinatown (a symbol of being a gang leader), gambling as he typesets for the San Francisco Chinese Times, working at the Oakland naval shipyards until the end of the war. He didn't get to stay on because he "didn't know enough English." My ignorant uncle Jose from Peru was to later say of me, "If I know a bellyful of English like you, I can fly!" Yes, it always looks easier from the outside.

"Those professors got so many degrees after their name it is like a monkey with many tails," said my dad, as he hoisted the cleaver high up and wacked down on the pork spareribs. I don't know what a professor makes, but I make 30-thou." Years later I learned that the restaurant's revenue is supposedly $100,000 a year and he *skimmed* $30,000 off the top, and still later on, I learned that he *cooked* the books. So, I never really know how much money there was that my mother was left with.

But I don't care anymore. After all, jackals eat corpses. We sleep in the bed that we made. He produced and trained the sons that would cheat his widow, cheat her to the point that she would go and ask her *mentally ill son* to manage her finances. I refused because I *was* mentally ill and because I was helping our cousins from the village in China, who were to take part in this capitalist environment.

Money grows here faster than rice back in China as they all assumed. And so to make enough money to satisfy their greed they would lose their identity in the process. To reclaim it, they go to a Chinatown restaurant and reserve tables for a banquet. That way, even the dishwasher gets to eat. Still, I was not there. I was homeless. Besides, I was not really myself, I was truly screaming "hysterically naked."

Watercress, that semi-aquatic green vegetable good for salads and said to thin your blood, seems to grow and thrive wherever they are tossed where there's mud and running water, is how the Chinese propagate. All the Chinatowns in the world seem to be a little village in China, a microcosm of xenophobic groups who don't seem to move fast enough because they haven't much to eat. But when they can, they gather at banquets that serve up to a thousand people when there is a wedding, birth, and sometimes even after a funeral. It all seems to ask: symbolically they seem to ask of each other, "Can we count on you sometimes when the chips are down?"

Our Locke Family Association in Seattle used to meet annually at the Sun Ya Restaurant in Seattle Chinatown. Our attendance exceeds 500 people. It starts with a couple of distinguished-looking Chinese professorial types welcoming the New Year, be it the Rabbit or the Snake, in poetry recited in Cantonese. How the hell did they get here, I would muse to myself. We are Toishanese, not city slickers. But they would have the podium and the microphone. Then one of their sons, some long-haired dude, would yell out in English, "Hey, Dad, speak plain English. We can't understand you!"

It is all rigged. They have the money. And so they naturally think that they are the leaders. Yeah, they are well-educated in Mencius and Kung Fu Tse, but their erudition to us cooks and waiters, you know, *ruhow* people, that are, reckless, uneducated people, seems that they are bragging about their useless sixth finger. They hold a small brush with black ink to paint birds and flowers on a scroll, whereas we "write big characters" with a mop on the floor. But if you rack their fingers a little bit, they will own up that they exploit their own people. And that's just what the white officials want - a model minority that can take care of itself. Chinese gambling, Chinese prostitution, loan-sharking, money-laundering, protection racketeering are left alone because of the "tolerance policy." There might be a philosophical justification for this. It is in the speech that these suited-men are delivering. "You can come to Chinatown and see the Hollywood façade of the pagodas and dragons-climbing on lamp posts, but you will not see the shithouse that the rear of the restaurants which really are there, and the poor cooks and kitchen help are kept way past their bed time cooking for the rest of the city - because the city has to eat before they do.

When I came over from China, I was a little smuggler at age 11. Sewn into my tailor-made suit at the waist were gold and jade. Their rubbing my waist made me itch on the plane but it was not feasible to scratch myself and so I endure the discomfort as Mount Fuji came into view. I deduced that the white cap on the mountain must be what they called "snow." Anyway, I carried enough valuables so that it paid for my airfare. And wouldn't you know it, I kept a fairly calm countenance throughout the trip so far. Then the old Chinese ladies told me to get off the plane here in Tokyo for dinner. The fried chicken dinner and orange juice was part of the itinerary. I was slightly air sick, as I was also susceptible to car and sea sickness. I couldn't eat but I drank the cold orange juice. I was alone. It was a crowded airport. I was alone and felt like an orphan.

I realized suddenly I was lost. Which? Which plane is mine? When will it take off? I was in a panic as I spoke neither Japanese nor English. I flagged down an airport worker and I asked him in Mandarin Chinese whether he can speak Chinese? He was bemused but concerned. He took out a pen and wrote on a pad of paper the characters for China. I nodded. Then a lucky guess on his part - he wrote down USA with a question mark. I nodded vigorously. He then look up to the Departures on the wall and wrote down the plane number and time for me. I only had 15 minutes left to be onboard. Otherwise they might have kept me in Japan and teach me how to make Sushi until my parents would come and ransom me.

Golden Dragon Massacre:

"Someone is singing Lord, Kumbaya…"

If I told you that there were no lows in my life that would be an utter lie. There were valleys and abysses. Upon my release from Napa, my father put me in the Chinatown YMCA. "I stayed here once too," he said, "and there is a swimming pool." Looking back thirty-six years in time, I realize why he paid my rent there. No one was willing to take me in anymore. They deemed me a danger or perhaps a pariah. When they needed me, I came, but once when I am in a jam, they threw away the sandwich. Then my father asked me how much money Benson gave me and what kinds of clothes I got.

"He never gave me any money," I told my father.

"I gave him $2,000. He must have paid $1,000 for your suit and shoes and had tea with his friends with the other $1,000."

I had a back payment of $1,400 from Social Security for SSI and so I had money to play the pinball machines alone at night at a joint that was opened all night. Maybe it was a "shooting gallery." I talked to no one and no one talked to me, except there was a guy that was also released from Napa. I invited him to my YMCA room and I had to go to the bathroom, and when he left I discovered something was missing, and I can't even remember what it was now but I know the guy took it. I got mad and bashed the guitar that Benson gave me "to assuage my loneliness." The smashed guitar resembled a de-gutted person with all the strings shooting out like intestines. I said to the guy when he visited again, "Here, I will give you my guitar, you can have it repaired." He never came back again.

I knew that Benson had many friends. His family used to kick ass in Chinatown. He and his brothers were "look-see boys." He lived with my parents in Aberdeen before he joined the Air Force. My father is his maternal uncle. My mother had fond memories of him because he was a practical joker and talked her into having a steak, and later on she found out it was horsemeat.

While at the YMCA, I heard some guy whistling "The East is Red." The year was 1977, a year after the fall of the I-Hotel when 500 policemen evicted low-income tenants in the middle of the night. That story even made the New Yorker.

My daily routine consisted of waking up and going to a bakery for pastries and tea in Waverly Lane half a block from the Y. At lunch, I go to some cheap café and order rice rolls with small shrimps and green onion embedded in it. I can't even tell you very much what I did because it was a blur. Here I was essentially abandoned by my family and relatives again, like a discarded tampon. Perhaps the lack of social outlets and dog-eat-dog living in the inner cities engendered gangs in Chinatown that no one likes to admit up to that time. That is, until the Golden Dragon Massacre.

I had met a homeless guy Steve who was playing his guitar in Chinatown after my arrest and going to Napa. I allowed him to sleep in my room in the day time. One morning as soon as I got out of the door, he came rushing to me and blurted out, "The Chinatown Mafia has gone nuts, and they just shot and killed a bunch of people in a restaurant."

As he calmed down, I realized that that accounted for all the ambulances I heard at 3 AM, and it sounded like twenty or thirty of them. Upon further inquiry, it was at the Golden Dragon Restaurant in Waverly Lane, only a half of a block away.

It was a chaotic time and I don't think I was hooked up with any mental health agency at the time. My social worker, Lloyd, who handled my case when I refused to talk to police and jail staff or lawyer before I was committed involuntarily to Napa, somehow found where I was living, and came to urge me to live in a halfway house, the Conard House. I went there and had dinner with the residents and I felt the reception was cool, too cool, and so I never went back to apply. Lloyd came back again and asked me why I didn't apply. I told him I did not fit the scene. "On the contrary, they liked you, and so you should apply." I applied. Mainly it was because the rent and one meal a day was only a third of my SSI income, when the YMCA took just about all my money.

The Third Floor Kitchen:

I wish I could talk to my mother again but she died on the last day of 1993 of blood cancer. Not that I need a mother now but I would like to apologize to her for her ignorance which never served me. Forward now in time to 2015 the penultimate month of cold rain and drafts. I am living in a first floor basement apartment with a roommate. We each have a room, yes, Virginia Woolf, we are grownups. But at Conard we had to share a room.

Alan Arkeley was my first roommate there and he was a lone photographer of lonely seascape and rear views of alleyways. He was tall and lanky. I slept most of the day. I had pathological anxiety. My brain felt like it was going to explode. To endure fifteen seconds of the excruciating tension was unbearable already beyond human endurance. Yet I was expected to do normal things a normal person would do.

Let anxiety be the thread then, but we will come back to the third floor kitchen of Conard House. Before any potentiality or opportunities arise, there are ways to castrate you without castrating you. Chemically. You know the joke when you go to the men's latrine. "Don't look up here for any (graffiti) jokes; you are holding it in your hand." I told Doctor Ron Smothermon that the medicine made me impotent. He said, "Well, have you got a girl friend?" I said no. And he said he will change it by and by when I had a girl friend.

Loraine was studying in a poetry MFA program on scholarship at Mills College in Oakland. She saved up a hundred pills of Trilafon and swallowed them in class. They had to pump her stomach. She showed me a poem she wrote and it was looking for father. The night counselor Harry introduced us and said, "Loraine is also from Seattle." That was all it took before I found out her father lived on Vashon Island and made jewelry. I called her "Angel" and asked her what she did all day. She told me she played the harp.

Now let's back up a little bit. I was the richest resident of Conard House. Why? Or How? I had a CETA scholarship to Cogswell College in Safety Engineering and I graded math papers and tutored physics and I also had SSI payments. Dick Telford taught physics and I was also tutoring it to fellow CETA students. Dick came to class late one day and explained that he was late because there was a leak of the shower stall the floor above him in the rooming house. That day they also switch me to a new medication. I asked Telford if I could take the test later. He said just try to take it and see what happens. And so I got an 80%. Another time Dick told us that he once dated a girl called Maryanne, and he said to her, "Maryanne, do you know what your father do in the Army?" She didn't know. And so Dick told her. "He wraps nails around a grenade and toss it into the middle of a herd of sheep and see how many get killed." Maryanne never responded to his calls after that, he said.

Dick told me he hated his mother and that's why he was so depressed, and that he took medication himself. He lectured me about meds. "Take it exactly as your doctor tells you, and don't drink or take street drugs." He had a Master's degree in physics at UC Berkeley and he told me he was also from Seattle. I remember his ads for tutoring in the UW Daily, the student newspaper at the UW in Seattle. He told me he made a good living since he didn't report his cash income for taxes.

I was a transient among transients in this world we called life, though the dead have undoubtedly outnumbered us. I saw Mt. Fuji in the distance and covered by what I assumed to be snow. That was my first snow - albeit from a distance.

(The Aberdeen Years)

The Aberdeen Years (A memoir fragment by Koon Woon)

The Madam's name was Sally. Just Sally, not Mustang Sally. The cover was a restaurant named The China Doll. Now after all these years, I think that my father was a partner in this house of prostitution.

One day in the early afternoon in Mr. Fare's 7th grade English class at Hopkins' Junior High in Aberdeen, I got called in the Intercom to go to the Principal's office. Mr. Fare was a blind former engineer who now taught English. He gave the lectures but his wife corrected the homework at home. I was a little nervous walking down the hallway. I was only fourteen at this time and I had been in the U.S. less than three years from China. But when I got to the Principal's office, the only thing waiting for me was the telephone. The Principal said that my father was on the phone.

I picked up the phone and my father said, "Don't be afraid; I am just calling you on the telephone." We were speaking Chinese.

"I am not afraid; I am just winded coming to the Principal's office."

"Good. Here's what I want you do to. Right after school, you go home and get bus money from your mother and take bus to Montesano to help me at the restaurant."

At that time in 1962, we sardined in the housing project in the West End of Aberdeen, WA. There were ten of us living in a three-bedroom duplex. Our only source of income was my father's employment as a cook. He had been working at the Smoke Shop restaurant owned by the mayor of Aberdeen as a breakfast cook when all of a sudden Sally offered him a job at the China Doll in Montesano, some ten miles east of Aberdeen.

[Forward in time 50 years - How did Sally come to have a restaurant named China Doll? Was it already a Chinese restaurant or at least it served Chinese food, for certainly the Chinese wok stoves were there in place. My siblings and I were too young --- maybe have this as conversation with Marv at the end of the book]

So, here I come, after running half a mile home from school and getting fifty cents from my mother for the bus. She had been told that I was required to come to help my father. I went to the bathroom and I was out of the door.

It was a spring afternoon, still a bit chilly, the smell of pulp and sawdust was in the air in this logging town. I waited for the bus alone on Simpson Avenue. Feeling a bit nervous but didn't know what to expect, I was glad when the bus arrived and I hopped on.

The China Doll was in the heart of downtown Montesano. An excuse of a town, with two or three main streets as I remember but it was the county seat of Grays Harbor. I had no trouble finding the restaurant. Its decor was an old saloon restaurant that you see in old Western movies. It was dimly lit by orange filament bulbs; a player piano on the right of the dining room, a jukebox, wooden tables and chairs, and on the left, a whiskey bar. I hesitated near the door. A middle-aged woman hurried out from the back, fleshy but not overweight; there was quite a bit of color on her cheeks, and she appeared to be a little Hispanic. Later, I found out that she was part Mexican. She was dressed in a gaudy red Chinese blouse.

"Honey, you must be Bill's son, aren't you?" She asked me as she approached. I said yes. She told me to go to the kitchen and my father will explain what I was supposed to do.

My father was stirring a pot of brown gravy behind the steam table as I went into the kitchen. He took one look at me and said, "We got lots work and so you fix yourself something to eat. Find it in the walk-in box and rice is already cooked.

I grilled three strips of bacon and fried two eggs and put them on top of steamed rice and sprinkled some soy sauce over it. My father told me to go and eat in the backroom behind the kitchen.

As I was eating, I recalled how just two years earlier, in Hoquiam, WA, my father and "Uncle Harry" partnered in the China Star Café. My brother Hank and I were just little boys

(Here's to Uncle Harry)

Uncle Harry

Hoquiam, WA, early 60's: 5 cent cigars from Bitar's, water melons

One Indian-head nickel per pound, silver dollars slapped down on bars,

Logs floating down the brackish Hoquiam River as tavern lights

Begin burning in low-blood-sugar afternoons. Uncle Harry, older than

My father and shorter than me, lies in bed in the Emerson Hotel:

The earth, flat before Columbus, is my ceiling and right about

Where the electrical pipe falls perpendicularly away is the land mass

Of Asia, my village, my house, a day's swim away to my wife, a shout away.

She's so winsome I married her against my mother's wishes. I had to

Chase the old woman with a pistol to convince her of my choice.

As Uncle Harry lay in bed, Hank and I climbed the dark stairs,

Pretending it was a haunted house. I knocked and Uncle Harry

Came to the door in yellowed briefs, smelling like the beer bottles

Hank finds with slugs inside. Embarrassed that my father has already

Cooked the chop suey, Uncle Harry coughed out, "Boys, I will come

Quickly to work." Inside his hotel room with the naked bulb, he

Is reminded of the interrogation at Angel Island, where he and

Other immigrants arriving from the Pacific were interned. He felt

Like a bug trapped in a child's matchbox:

Language box you, color box you, heritage box you, politics box you.

Shaving my thin, yellow cheeks. How I would like to see my son now,

His cheeks fat! The Hotel stairs are steep and dark,

A man needs his son to holler out the false steps.

I pay by the month but there'll be no record of me being here.

A man needs a son to write down his legacy, which is transitory

As the summer span of an insect, which lands and then takes off again.

Now back at the backroom of the China Doll, as soon as I dished myself a plate of rice, my father criticized me for not eating enough. "It is going to be long night," he said, "you are going to need work hard." I was never robust as a child though. Malnutrition in China in my boyhood years made me thin and weak and a bit bowlegged, with spine curvature from the lack of calcium. As soon as I finished eating, my father asked me to peel a big pot of boiled potatoes and make a huge mound of hash browns. The menu had steaks and chops besides chop suey and egg foo young. Later, I discovered that there's a small oven that they baked pizza slices. But the real business, as I was to discover later, was upstairs. There was a little button to alert the "girls," who doubled up as waitresses, so that a customer, or "john," was coming up. That button was hidden under a little humorous sign, which had something written on it to the effect that "No one minds if you have an beer for an eye-opener in the morning, a bloody Mary or two to take care of a hangover, then a drink or two to wash down your lunch, a thirst quencher in the middle of the afternoon, and a drink with dinner, and a martini to relax in the evening, and throw in a glass of wine for relaxation or for entertainment in company, nobody minds if you do it in moderation, but this goddamn business of sip, sip, sip business all day long has got to stop!"

The side work in a restaurant is endless. This was in the late afternoon about 4 o'clock, as my father and I were already frantically trying to get the side work done. He had been apparently roasting a chunk of beef in the oven. He puts celery and onions in the pan and he pokes hole with a knife so that he could put cloves of garlic inside the meat. He also salts it and peppers it. He also had me make a pot of mashed potatoes. Then I was in the back doing the usual Chinese chop suey prep work - peeling onions, celery, cutting Napa cabbage and mincing pork. I can't remember whether we had bean sprouts or not at that time. At that time, in the early 60's, each individual Chinese restaurant had to grow its own beans sprouts. Nowadays, it is available in most supermarkets. And commercial beans sprout growers make deliveries to restaurants every day.

My father had tons of things to do. He had to make sweet and sour spareribs, fried rice, egg foo young, while I had to make batter for the deep-frying. He fortified himself by coffee and cigarettes. We were preparing for the combination dinners. But we didn't have the Bob Hope joke dinner, "With four, you get egg roll." Those days there were no egg roll wrappers and you actually had to make your own wrappers out of eggs and flour in the wok and it was very delicate work. My father was able to do it, since he had worked in large, fancy restaurants in San Francisco, before he moved to Aberdeen, where his Uncle Benny Locke was. He moved to Aberdeen because he was planning a family, after my mother immigrated to America in 1951. He didn't want his children growing up in S.F. and becoming gang members.

According to my father, Benny Locke treated him very shabbily at the Canton Café in Aberdeen, which is still there, now operated by Benny Locke's grandson, Garcia. Back in the 1940's when America was at war in World War II, everyone was employed in factories, producing war goods and accessories, with some men getting a lot of women, because so many had been absent as soldiers. The war economy benefited Benny Locke. He had employees in his restaurant.

My father had worked for Benny for several years and was mistreated. He had to work the longest hours and he got the least pay. He was exploited to put it simply. That's because he had several children one child after another, because there was no birth control at that time. And Benny would blatantly say to people, when my father complained about his unfair treatment, "Where is he going to go? He's got so many kids hanging onto him like grapes." This was in reference to a famous saying by a jade carver in Chinese history.

A noble once asked a jade carver to carve him a mansion out of a large piece of jade. Back in those historical times, the jade carver had to meditate on what's inherent in the jade stone. He told the noble that he didn't see a mansion but only a bunch of grapes. The implication is that the grapes will also be sour. And so Benny was saying that my father was jealous of the other relatives who worked for Benny.

But there's always the straw that breaks the camel's back. One Christmas, the crew still had to work for Benny at the Canton Café. After closing, they had a dinner party. Benny had my father grill steaks for everyone. But as everyone had sit down to eat, Benny picked the smallest of all the steaks and put it on my father's plate. The years of humiliation and exploitation came to a head. My father gave the steak to the waitress and ***walked out into the night.***

Now back at the China Doll, I was peeling prawns and halving them and de-veining them. People started coming in for dinner. Sally the Madam went upstairs through the stairs from a side door in the kitchen to get the "girls" to come down to wait on tables.

I remember that there were three "girls" who doubled- up as waitresses. They were all dressed in tight slacks and blouses. My father asked me, after the girls had come down, whether I see anything peculiar about these girls. I said no, even though I knew better.

The girls were named "Ginger," "Susie," and "Lee." Ginger was the oldest, around 30. Lee was around 24 and Susie, the one I liked the best, was around 20, because later on, she helped me wash dishes at closing time.

There were just my father and I in the kitchen. He had to cook for maybe 60 people if the place all filled up, and I helped as frantically as I could. But you know how the saying goes – "If you can't stand the heat, get out of the kitchen." The pressure of a fry cook was tremendous on my father, and he would shout and scream at me to hurry up as the evening went on, when we were putting out orders. I presumed that's what it would be like in the military.

Just remember that I had probably been up since seven in the morning and I had a full day of school and now I am working into the wee hours of the night, when the restaurant closes at two in the morning, and then there's an hour of cleaning up, washing dishes and so forth. But Friday night wasn't the worst. Saturday night was worse, because after my father drove us home at three in the morning I would not be able to sleep except for a couple of hours because of all the tension at the restaurant, and the fact that my siblings would be getting up shortly and begin a day of noise. Then Saturday afternoon at two in the afternoon, my father and I return to the China Doll. And then we don't get home until three o'clock Sunday morning.

The worst wasn't the physical exertion, but it was the psychological harm. At that time, the Prime Minister of England was caught with a call girl named Christine Keeler. And it was international news even in our local newspaper. The whorehouse was a buzzed with this news. Unfortunately, those two experiences - the whorehouse and the girls, and Christine Keeler and the spies - got mixed up in my head, and I was never going to trust a woman again after that, because I think that every woman is a spy. Illogical, but that's how the mind connects.

Sally the madam paid me a dollar an hour for work. And so I made twenty-two dollars a week, and my parents allowed me to keep the money. The first thing that I purchased was a tape recorder. As I was showing the tape recorder to my mother in my father's presence in the house we lived in on Oak Street in Aberdeen, she said to my father, "It's good that he has learned the value of money." At that time, I didn't appreciate the extent of her need for money and her greed for it. It was another 10 years before I was rudely awakened to her miserliness.

One would expect that sooner or later the whorehouse would have troubles. First the police started coming to interview Lee. I didn't know what her problems were. Eventually, Sally had to close shop, but before she could leave town, she had to pay off the sheriff. She stayed at our cramped quarters in our house in the housing project for a few days. It was somehow decided that my father would get all the restaurant equipment. These included the wok stoves and the American oven and grill. This equipment were moved somehow from Montesano ten miles to Aberdeen, where my father had bought a hamburger drive in called Vic's Burgers on Simpson Avenue. And with an interest-free loan from a relative we started our own restaurant again. It was the birth of the Hong Kong Café.

I remember going to the little Hong Kong café and getting the kitchen started before my mother would come as waitress in the summers beginning at age sixteen. This was to give my father a couple more hours of sleep, while my mother and I opened the restaurant. Typically, I would make brown gravy, chicken noodle soup, cook rice, and make sweet and sour spareribs and a batch of chop suey, all of which would go on the steam table. Those days I was motivated to help my family.

The Slow Hours In the slow hours of the café, I read books. My father would work in the kitchen and I would be out waiting on tables. My mother didn't come to work until about six in the evening, as she had the responsibility of the household with a husband, eight children and herself. My father and I would come to work about two in the afternoon. I would don on my white waiter's jacket, fill the soy sauce, black pepper, salt, sugar, and napkin holders and clean the ashtrays from the previous night. I would make tea in the urn and make a pot of fresh coffee. After those and other side work, I would sit quietly in a booth and read books.

We would only have a stray customer or two until about four thirty or five o'clock, when people start coming in to eat dinner. This was in the summer time, when there was the sunshine of honey outside and the quiet hum of the beer and wine cooler kept me company inside.

In my teenage years from sixteen onto my early twenties when I came home from college in the summers, I would get into this routine. I was waiting for the world to happen. And sadly, it never did open up for me, due to my bipolar illness in my mid-twenties. But that's a story for later. For now, it is the story of the waiter.

The first book that made me cry I remember was Charles Dickens' Oliver Twist. But I did not feel that I had any sensitivity to literature. I was more interested in reading philosophy. I read Nietzsche, John Locke, Marx, Schopenhauer, Wittgenstein, John Wisdom (who was my philosophy teacher at the University of Oregon) and a host of analytic philosophers.

Although I was appointed literary chairman in my senior year at Aberdeen high school, my father did not allow me to stay after school to participate. So, all the teenage years were just school, work, and reading whenever I could get it in. I would also read books of a practical nature. I read books on buying and selling stocks, economic history, and even Mao Tse Tung's books on literature and contradictions. My mind was bombarded with both Eastern and Western ideas, as I read the Tao Te Ching and Freud in one breath.

There was one girl who came in alone and sometimes with her sister. She usually sat alone and drank black coffee in the slow hours of the restaurant. She had these dark Spanish eyes. My parents disapproved of me flirting with girls. And like an obedient first-born son and China born besides, I was expected to someday marry a Chinese girl from Hong Kong and take over the family restaurant. I didn't even know her name. She was only about a year older than I was and she wasn't in school. Although she had been coming for two or three years since I was a sophomore in high school, she was always alone, without a boy friend. She said she lived alone although she had a mother. She said that her mother let her be on her own if she didn't get into trouble.

Now at the age of fifty-six, I still remember her and the sadness I felt that I had to think about geometry and Cartesian coordinates instead of dating a white girl. My family controlled me to the very last detail of my toilet article. And slowly I developed anxiety from the lack of relief and the need to get out as in a spaceship from a dying planet. I wrote this poem, thinking of that girl, and I sure as hell wished that she found happiness and was not a depressive:

Anxiety

I shall spend the rest of my years

climbing, in order to come down the mountain

as a white-beard.

I have closed doors –

rooms I won't go back to.

I have seen myself sitting
in the lobby of the Emerson Hotel, looking out
seeing young lasses and saying to myself,
"They would decorate my room very well."

A memory snags me –
the woman with Spanish eyes,
sitting at the same coffee counter
also drinking black coffee
and not a word was exchanged.
The pain of wild flowers in a city ravine.

I bought and sold. Sold and bought.
In the end, I didn't gain.
My hotel was managed once by Franz Kafka.
A room with a typewriter at one corner.

Despite false alarms, pinto beans
and bacon rinds sustain me,
as I listen to the hiss of radiator steam.
Unfortunately, the hotel only keeps

its registry for so long.

There will not be a record of me.

The earthmovers and the cranes

are now just across the street.

It fills me with anxiety,

because I have read ahead in the book,

and seen the end from the beginning.

-

"The Tao that can be told is not the Tao.
The name that can be named is not the name."

The gold dust of Californ' lured my ancestors from China to Gim Shan (America). But when they arrived, the gold was gone. So, they built railroads. My great-grandfather settled in the town of Hoquiam in Washington State and provided support to the logging and lumber industries. He owned a laundry and shares in restaurants. His English was excellent. The Mayor of Hoquiam approached him, "Hey, Locke Li, I need 500 men to get the trees out of Humtulips. How about if I go with you to your village and bring back 500 healthy, strong men to build a section of railroad?"

So, off they went and did that, as my father told me that about a hundred years later in the kitchen of our Chinese-American restaurant. I have myself investigated the woods and bramble in Humtulips, just north of Hoquiam and I found abandoned rail tracks. Other people are rumored to have found discarded opium bottles. Opium was a pain killer. It killed the pain of "bitter strength" for these "indentured servants," who could neither own property nor bring their wives and families over from China, and they were forbidden to marry white women. My father would be telling me this as he sipped from a bowl of boiled vinegar. My father in some ways reminded me of Fidel Castro, who could "out shoot, out fight, and out con anybody." But he really wasn't like that when his guard is down at home. His wife cuts his hairs and buys slacks for him.

The 500 or so of the Locke's that came over from Toishan, our county in China, eventually settled down in all the small towns of Washington state in Aberdeen, Elma, Centralia, Olympia and Seattle and east of the mountains in Yakima and Wenatchee, and then later, when they had a bigger purses, settled in other states such as California, Arizona, Michigan, and New York. Most of them were in the restaurant business and so they had to move apart because otherwise they'd be in direct competition with each other.

Everything starts at the Last Exit, short for the Last Exit on Brooklyn, which was a freeway exit and what Lenny Bruce made famous with his comedy gig on a radio broadcast. He was prosecuted for profanity, the same way that Allen Ginsburg's book *Howl* was first banned because of profanity charges. The Exit, as we called it short for The Last Exit on Brooklyn, was on Brooklyn Avenue, one street down from the "Ave," or the University Way, which is the main street of the University District, which is the commercial street next to the campus of the University of Washington on the northern side. The University District runs down to the canal, a man-made channel that connects the two lakes in Seattle - Lake Washington and Lake Union. The Last Exit was pretty close to the bottom of the hill, as if all the dregs would drift this way on a rainy day. For 10 years, I was a sitter at the Last Exit, I kept the wooden bench warm, sometimes playing chess and sometimes playing Go, but most of the time was not engaged in "productive" behavior.

Jose

Here is a man who has traveled and lived on three continents, only to die alone in a desolate North American hotel room. Not that he didn't have family; families he had two of his own, one in Hong Kong and one in Peru. But his spouses only gave him illegitimate children.

My uncle Jose always leaves a trail of water and bits of vegetables when he worked in the restaurant kitchen. Similarly, he left unfinished business and traces of himself where he had traveled and lived. He walked unevenly because one of his legs was shorter than the other. Born in China, immigrated to Peru at an early age, and came to Washington State when sponsored by his sister at the age of fifty, he died alone in a hotel room meant for an overnight guest in Seattle's Chinatown. Is there something that attracted people to come to Seattle's Chinatown, a most comatose place in the entire cosmos, or is it simply bad *feng shui*?

When Jose first arrived, he and I shared the old house on Bay Avenue, across the dirt field beyond which lies the rail tracks. Freights with cargo came from Georgia on the Georgia Pacific line to the Port of Grays Harbor in Aberdeen, where in the past, lumber was shipped to Japan. In exchange of lumber to build houses in earthquake-ridden Japan, we purchased the latest in consumer electronic gadgets from there.

My mother is Jose's younger sister. When our small family-owned café in the small town of Aberdeen expanded when tourism was still good, my father needed an extra hand in the kitchen. So we sponsored Jose over from Peru. Jose claimed to have worked in big *chifas* in Peru that served over a thousand people. After some familiarity with her oldest brother, whom she has not seen since she was six in China, my mother, between dinner and bar rush, would say, "Take back your wife, Poi's mother, so that you will have someone to take care of you in old age and burn incense for you in *the after.*"

"But I didn't adopt Poi," Jose would protest, "That woman did herself," referring to his legal wife in China.

"It is too late to argue such matters," my mother would speak a bit louder over the cracking of the hot oil in the frying wok, "Your foreign Peru woman is a foreign devil. At least your wife in China is Chinese." To this Jose had no reply. He was over fifty with a limp and dependent on his sister's family for work and company. None of them were sympathetic to his life's choices. And Jose couldn't speak English, although fluent in Chinese and Spanish.

The night that Jose died in his room at the Republic Hotel in Chinatown, Doctor Hong signed Jose's death certificate. His Peruvian wife Carmen said that she and my uncle Jose went shopping the previous day and Jose had fallen on the escalator. That's why his body was all bruised up. My mother didn't pay for the funeral and burial and so Jose got a pauper's grave. I didn't even know which cemetery. My mother had not talked to me for some time and I found out about Jose's death from my brother Lange. Lange is the bearer of bad news, as well as good news, I suppose, because he is the bearer of all news. That was his function in the family. He had the gift of gab. The rest of us did whatever work was in front of us – chopping onion, de-veining prawns, whipping gravy, or ladling soup. Lange had polio in one arm and so he waited on the customers. Since none of us got paid when we worked for our family in our teen years, Lange worked for tips. So, Lange became a "smooth talker," as our family friend Marvin the Sears and Roebuck mechanic would say.

He spins it just right is the way I saw how he operated. My sister Linda said that Lange was just "happy-go-lucky." My siblings all seem to speak a different language than I did, because I was born in China, the same as my parents. My parents referred to my siblings as "jook sing" or bamboo-natured, because they were like bamboo, hard and sturdy outside, but wildly hollow inside. So, I got the burden of being the Number-One-Son. It is just some unfair game my parents played on guys like Jose and me.

"I don't know how much professor makes, I make thirty thou," is what my father says to me. I had wanted to be a mathematician ever since I saw an inspirational film about a mathematician and how goes about doing his work. The film showed a mathematician; just a man dressed casually bending over a creek and looking intently at the flow of the water. He then draws arrows on his clipboard and scribbled some letters and numbers. He is representing the water flow by a vector field. These are a bunch of short arrows that depict the direction and force of the water flow. This way he could calculate the erosion on the creek bank over time. He makes a representation of the real world with a set of diagrams and formulas. He just needed a clipboard and a pen. I thought to myself, "Wow, that's a job I like - work alone, anywhere, see things out there and inside your head. And you don't have to be in a shop or an office. That would be the ideal job for me!" And I did well in high school. But my father had other plans for me and was out to sabotage me. At least, that's what my paranoia ideation tells me now. Today I am 62 years old and my father has been dead for 25 years, a quarter of a century. And my wife tells me that I am still talking about my father as though he was in the bedroom with us. But what my parents did tell me though, one night after the closing hour of the restaurant, they took out a jade and gold set. It was an investment. They are from the old country and never trust the value of currency and so they invested in jewelry. And the Chinese value jade the most.

My mother holds up a jade bracelet. Even I was surprised at the color composition of the jade. It appeared to be milkfish with different hues of different colors diffusing in the stone, as if an orange or blue cloud would disperse and spread in the sky. "You hold up a piece of jade to the sky," my mother said, "it is looks like clouds running in the jade, then it is good jade," she said.
"Someday when we can't see you anymore, you will have some jade too," said my dad. He was wearing a soft green sweater, as if that softened him as well. That was a benign time when I was 21 years old, back from the University of Oregon, visiting for the Christmas holiday. Later on times did not prove to be so bucolic.

During the summers that I am home from the University of Oregon in Eugene, I donned on the waiter's yellow jacket, do the side work filling the soy sauce bottles, which are dark and brooding like Nietzsche, next to the white salt shakers and the pepper, a shade in between. I would wipe the already clean table tops, make an urn of Oolong tea and a pot of Simonson's coffee, I would sit quietly at a booth and read my philosophy books. The weather out is gorgeous but I could only see Mr. Beesaw's hotel across the street and occasionally, Amie, who is Taiwanese married to Beesaw when he was in the US Navy stationed in Taipei. She cleaned the rooms while Beesaw was a buyer for the new House of Value a few blocks away on Myrtle Street, the dividing line between Aberdeen and Hoquiam.

We are on Simpson Avenue, which is coastal highway 101 going through Aberdeen and Hoquiam and we are just 3 blocks south of Hoquiam. So, one time, a very well dressed, basketball player type of a black man stepped inside the café. My brother John was with me, at the cash register, as the stranger approached. "Hey brother," he said, "I am here to raise money for bibles for our brothers at Monroe." Monroe is a state penitentiary. He spoke clearly and to the point. "Our brothers need something to read to pass the time. Can you help?" I looked at John and he looked at me. What it looked like was that even if John and I fight the guy, we would get the worse of it, as there is no one in the café but us. Our parents had gone to Seattle for the day to buy special Chinese groceries for family use.

"I am just the manager," I said, "and I can't make money decisions like those." He took a step forward and I am glad that there was the counter between us.

"Look brother, I have obtained special permission to do this." He took out a letter written on police department stationery. He thrust it to me to read. I read it carefully and slowly. I shook my head.

"Why are you shaking your head? Our brothers need the word of God to guide them through slow, difficult times."

"I am unable to help you," I said. I looked at my brother John who was visibly nervous. The black man let out a sigh and looked at John and said, "Is he your brother? I have a letter here signed by the Chief of Police that permits us to solicit on behalf of our brothers doing time." John took a step backward. He was trained in Gungfu but 130 pounds is no match for some ex-marine-looking dude. He was easily over six feet in his stocking feet and naked on the bathroom scale registering 250. John quickly looked back at me, with his eyes pleading. I stood my ground, "I am unable to help you," I said again. The boss isn't here and I am unable to make decisions to give to charity.

"O man, all we are asking is $40 bucks for some bibles," he said indignantly but more negotiable.

"I am sorry, my friend. We are in business and the rule says that I cannot make decisions that I don't have the authority to," I said without any quivering in voice or varied my stance. I stood squarely in front of him separated by the coffee counter. I think he could still throw a punch at me with his long arm and the punch may connect.

He stared at me with a sense of disgust and ultimately, a sense of disappointment. He turned to leave, and when he reached the door, he said, "Our brothers in prison will be disappointed not to be able to read the word of God."

When he was gone, John asked me, "Weren't you afraid of him?"

"Business is business. When in doubt, choose business. Business rules over everything else." I said. "Giving money away is not the way to do business. But you know what?"

"What?" said John.

"The guy didn't know he was in Aberdeen. The letter was signed by the Hoquiam Chief of Police. And we are over the border into Aberdeen. He didn't know the difference between Aberdeen and Hoquiam. He didn't know that Myrtle Street was the dividing line!

"Wow, I still would be afraid of him," John admitted.

There was the dark side too about my father and his business. He claimed to be a member of the Triad. He told me tales after the day is over at the restaurant.

3am tales from the restaurant kitchen:

The background was the Sino-Japanese War in the 1930's in China. People had to do more unethical things to survive and to prosper. My father was a young man of sixteen and he was a bookkeeper to an illiterate criminal in China.

That's what my father told me as we ate our closing meal together in the kitchen table. We sat on milk crates. It was 3AM. We had closed up Saturday night at 2AM and did all the cleaning up. Now it is our turn to eat, after the whole town of Aberdeen has eaten. In the simple fury of work, we neglected out needs.

With all the lights turned off except the one naked bulb by the walk-in refrigerator, my father pours soy sauce over his rib steak which lies on top of a mound of white rice on a steak platter. He seldom eats vegetables. I had stir-fried myself a plate of shrimp and garden vegetables and served it with white rice. First we ate in silence for a while. Then he began.

"I knew a guy then. He knew business. He even brought dog meat and sold it from village to village." My father took out a Marlboro cigarette from his white shirt pocket, lit it with a match, took a puff, and continued with his story, "but the guy was illiterate and I had went to high school and so he hired me for his bookkeeper." He paused and took a couple more puffs from his cigarette and cupped his left hand and used it as an ashtray, since we didn't keep an astray on the backroom table. He then told me that one time the criminal was desperate for money and had robbed an old woman. Later he went up to her and asked her if she remembered him. She said quite stupidly, " Of course! You are the dead-bag boy who robbed me of my grocery money! I hope you rot in hell." The criminal had no recourse but to murder her since he didn't want to be caught. But, my father, as he took his final puff on the Marlboro, said, "The guy was caught and hung." He said that without any comment. It was more or less a statement about the nature of the business enterprise.

I by this time realize that my chow har or stir-fried shrimp with vegetables had grown cold from listening to his story. It was indeed the dead of the night, time for plots and assassins to go about their business. Then suddenly my father changed the subject.

"Have you ever thought of business?" He asked. "You know, we are doing pretty good now. The bank says it will give me credit for a hundred thou. You can get your grandmother to pick a nice girl for you from Hong Kong. She will carry a purse and you can put things in it. You won't be so lonely and drift. When I was your age, I wasted a lot of time too. Until I went back and got your mom over. What you say?"

Just then the freight train whistled by a few blocks away. It was close to four a.m. and almost time for sleep, after a bath at the apartment the other side of the restaurant parking lot for me. Yes, I was beginning to feel a sense of losing direction. I no longer read Nietzsche with adolescent adoration. I still couldn't understand Logical Positivism. Mathematics no longer seems to satisfy my longing. I was to waste several years drinking, betting at the racetrack, and smoking dope until I would have a psychotic break with reality.

This was still a relatively benign time, but loneliness was eating me like a time bomb.

We finished eating. Our house is in the back of the restaurant. My mother usually doesn't eat at night with us and she's gone into the house to watch a late show on television or to wash her hair. I said good night to my father and walked across the parking lot of the restaurant to our apartment house where I had one of the three apartments.

I remember Uncle Harry who used to be partners with my father in Hoquiam. After closing, Uncle Harry would go to a bar and invariably drink until he passes out in the streets and then my father would have to bail him out of jail. Uncle Harry's wife was in China. And he had a sleeping room at the dusty Emerson Hotel. My brother Hank and I used to have to go and wake Uncle Harry up to come to work.

Well, my bath is ready. I will soak my tense and tired muscles. Smoke a couple of cigarettes in the tub. It was suffocating to be in Aberdeen after attending the University unsuccessfully. I was beginning to suspect that I was failing but I didn't know why or how to stop it or where to get help.

Dissatisfaction and Departures

Being one of five Chinese families who are all related and all in competition with each other operating Chinese restaurants, we did not much get along with each other. My parents did not allow me to socialize with anyone. I found solace only in the middle of the night playing chess out of a book. I was in all modesty fairly bright in academic subjects and had been in a "bright and gifted" seminar for high school students at Western Washington State College after my junior year in high school and was asked by M.I.T. to apply to them. But I really was not socially well-adjusted. I was lonely and I wanted to escape somehow the rigidity of a conservative logging and fishing town. This next poem aptly characterizes how I felt:

Aberdeen, 1966

Or, Driving Around for a Poem

Driving behind a logging truck with dancing flags
Pinned onto the logs, I listen to "Norwegian Wood"
Miss Freeland wants a poem for her creative-writing class.
In the Pulse of saw mills I cut this logging town
Into board-feet with my '55 Plymouth, with sawdust
Plenty to make ice-cream cones. I tend to forget
The manure that gives us Red Delicious, or this memory.

Between windshield-wiper swings I hear the tugs' blasts.
Perch and red snapper flap on Scandinavian boats.
Neighborhoods where I sold the *Reader's Digest*
In Finnish or Polish editions. Catching a glimpse
Of a girl at the S.H. Kress coffee counter, I think
Of the book on the backseat, *Eleven Kinds of Loneliness.*

The doctors in the antiseptic Backer Building can't take away

This and other pains of a small town.

It is near Xmas. My little brother peeks out the window

Of the car. He is promised hot dogs and ice-cream for coming along.

If a pretty girl raises her umbrella, I'll write a long poem.

No such luck. We cross over to Cosmopolis to see

Boys fishing the Wishkah for sturgeon.

The car is damp, the heater doesn't work.

In the monotony of rain and windshield-wiper swings

I think I have a rhythm to beat the words against.

My brother and I settle for hog dogs and milk shakes

At a drive-in going out of town.

Anther poem about departures from Aberdeen is the following:

Flight

Oak Street never had oaks: this much we knew
of the street we lived on. Aberdeen

In the encyclopedia refers you to Scotland.

You know,

Nineteen years of it is visual purple,

A shiver when you have the right answer in a high school math class,

A 35-pound salmon on a 20-lb. test, a 1909-S VDB penny.

The Rain Derby, to guess the year's rainfall to the nearest

hundredth of an inch, and

An occasional carnival keep he town buoyant,

Even though half of the graduating class leaves Aberdeen.

When they come to the Satsop River,

A slender body of water like a nun,

Never pregnant, not even in the rainy seasons,

They hesitate, but only momentarily, before pretending to be

Alexander the Great crossing the Tiber.

Channel cats (catfish) would either dig a hole

in the muddy bottom, lodge themselves, vacuum

All the food that drift their way, or swim downstream forever.

Hank keeps coming back to Aberdeen for his limit of razor clams

at Oyehut, to find

His poker luck at the Spar, to his ex-wife and two kids,

To bowl at the Harbor Lanes with Frank, the Taholah Judge,

To the blueberry shrubs only he knows where in the foothills of the Olympics.

To be sure, there are casualties in life, one such casualty is a fellow classmate who was the most promising of us of that graduating class. The following was what I had written about him:

The ignorance of the sea really bothers me. My "friend" in high school who had an IQ of 160 killed himself. Like me, he didn't have a friend. Aberdeen was not a good place for a Jew to grow up. Aberdeen boasted of its stinking pulp mills. It might have been Auschwitz for him.

Jerry Katz told me this. We meet by chance in an espresso place in an alley in the U-District. Katz, another misfit in high school, once barged in on us in the lunchroom where marginal guys and "bright" students sat and ate. We sort of resented his intrusion. I remember Katz being really aggressive and complained about everything. The other told me he was Jewish. I didn't at that time learn how to tell origins and ancestry by people's surnames. At that time, I didn't know what being Jewish meant except that it had something to do with Freud and Auschwitz where millions of Jews died. Millions of Chinese and Russians also died in World War II. I however admired the Jewish intellectuals and physicists such as Marx and Einstein.

"By the way," said Katz, after we decided to have another espresso, "do you know what happened to Tom?"

"The last I heard, he had married a girl from Taiwan and he was in graduate school at Harvard."

"He killed himself," Katz said almost gloatingly. But maybe "gloatingly" isn't the right word, but it seems to be some kind of competition trip that Katz and many of us were into at that time. "At least we are alive," said Katz.

I decided not to tell Katz of my mental illness. I decided that he wouldn't understand. Perhaps Tom would, but he is dead.

The light at the espresso place seemed dimmer to me all of a sudden and these mod-clod new wave stylistic people seemed to be wearing masks and gutless passions. And Katz was droning on how he wants to become a writer. He seemed to be enjoying himself I have to admit. His acne is a thing of the past.

"We are alive, and Tom is dead! Think of the irony!" Exclaimed Katz.

"The smart ones don't have a monopoly to life," I said quietly. But I don't think Katz had heard me.

"Koon, it is nice to run into you. I have to go and write."

I left the Allegro espresso place as soon as Katz did. *Tom, Aberdeen is what killed you your mother came to the counselor in high school and said y son has an IQ of 160 and I want the best possible education for him and the counselor told us that such a mother existed and we all knew who it was because you had some original research published in SCIENCE magazine when you were 16. I am not grieving you because we weren't that good of friends but I consider your death a tragedy and I somewhat understand because I never found nourishment in that hick town either. But I feel sorry for you because you didn't know how to survive; whereas with me, I've been locked up several times and forced to take medicine and I carry a mental atom bomb everywhere I go and I don't enjoy it, but I must endure.*

I remember in the Bellevue run for our gym class I shot out to pass everyone though many were jocks. It was a mistake on my part not to pace myself accordingly. Then I tired out and Logan, Cowan, Orr, and everyone else started to pass me as near the hills of Bellevue. I kept on going even though I developed stomach cramps and diarrhea. So during the final quarter Tom had caught up with me and he tried to pass. The one thought I had was just to take a shit in the bushes. Tom came closer and he had a tentative but determined look. He started to pass. I sprint away. This reminded me of what my Spanish teacher Mr. Crabb had told me, "If you have a toothache on the day of the IQ test, you are not going to register as being very smart." Tom's father, Dr. Osheroff, was a dentist. Tom in the run came up again and I said to myself, "Shit, I just want to take a shit!" I decided it wasn't so important who wins or loses anymore and I drew back. Tom passed me and he looked back, giving me what I thought was a look of gratitude.

What had happened was that in every honors class that I had been in, Tom had been there a year before. I joined the math club and there Tom was the president. One time the head of the data processing division of the college came to administer a programming aptitude test and I sat down to take it, sweat and all as I had just finished my mail run for the post office where I was working part time after school. I scored in the low "A" range and Jack Soloman gloated, "I scored higher than Koon Woon!" Later on Jack became a physicist. It was ok to knocked down Koon Woon once in a while, but nobody could touch Tom Osheroff. And twenty years later, Tom's surviving older brother Doug was to win the Nobel Prize in physics.

And it came to being that that Tom and I were in a calculus course together at the college at night because we had finished taking all the math courses our high school had to offer. I told Tom that I could commute with him since I had a car. We usually said very little during the ride as neither of us knew any small talk. The calculus instructor was Mr. Aleksy, who flew Allied bombings of Germany in World War II. I thought that Tom would never repeat himself, but he told me that several times. Aleksy to me was a petty little Republican golfer when I delivered his mail, as he practiced a putt on his front lawn. He told me that two senators had written letters of recommendation for his son to get into the Naval Academy. But I slept in his class because I was dog-tired. Tom was always showing Aleksy little theorems he had proved but the Allied Bomber wasn't impressed and Tom would turn to me and say, "Does this seem right to you?" Of course I hadn't got to that point yet.

One night as I was driving Tom to his house which was on the Bellevue hills my car engine overheated and I asked

Tom to bring me a bucket of water. His parents asked me to come in for a moment. They were playing cards. Mr. Osheroff had a public face in his dentist capacity at the Becker Building when I delivered his mail. That night it was the first time I had entered a professional man's home. Dr. and Mrs. Osheroff were kind enough to ask me a few perfunctory questions. I really felt a social class below them though and wished that my father knew more English. Tom told me that his Dad knew every science fiction book motif ever written. I couldn't tell him that my father was unable to read even one science fiction book.

Now, I am sitting at a coffee shop and I am thinking how a small town could kill. It didn't kill me but I developed mental illness. John Etelamaki had developed an ulcer in the eighth grade and went to work at the newspaper loading dock. He was thinking about winning a scholarship in the eighth grade. And then the social scene all three of us had missed. School dances and prom kings and queens. Now I think back on it – it was all very serious matter at the time. But now it was all silliness. I am sorry, Tom, that you took it all so seriously.

Now nearly four decades later, I don't understand any more of that than what I did then, but I wrote this poem, which expresses somewhat of my feelings:

Considering...

Considering the suicides...

Those days Sylvia and Ann, who took

phrases and turned them into life but took

their own lives and turned them into nothingness ---

all because there were not the little pills then.
But! Would they have the poetry
if the right pills existed for them?

But considering the depressives and how difficult
it is to get along with them,
I almost would not have them or their poetry.
And Lowell himself is a skunk
that haunts a bad neighborhood in the dead hours
of the night; I rather be dismissed and free.

I myself have toured the sewers of the city,
but instead of seeing myself in every tortured face,
I saw every tortured face as a face of its own.
And now I am on those little pills
that subdue fires and repair torn spaghetti that wires
the brain; I am told --- it does not matter,
life is better this way.

Considering the suicides, how short they lived,
even Roethke himself, whose music was drowned

carelessly before his philosophy,
I am glad that as a man from the unlikely sector,
I am able to offer a slice of tangerine,
after the torrid hours and the slow hours
in which the slough reversed its flow,
that across the bitter midnight investigations
of the mean city with its mean machines,
I have come back to you and make this report.

I have considered the suicides and their notes
and conclude that we all do this in various ways,
in ways that we veer away from humanity,
but I am glad that there is a doctor among us,
William Carlos Williams, who signs a plain
prescription: "Live!"
What more can I say? But to speak plainly of plain folks
and to feel sorry for the suicides who took themselves
way too seriously.

Because of the nature of my illness and because of my father's actual or suspected activities, I have facts or fiction that I don't really know the veracity of, but the following is what I had written to a fellow writer friend:

Dear joe,

I trust that you had a wonderful get together with your family for Thanksgiving.

I have realized that what my friend Dr. Laurence P. Jacobs have been telling me all these years about writing. The reason I am now able to think about writing a memoir is that I am beginning to work through my life-long Paranoia ideation which is a part of my personality as well as my mental illness. I was first paranoid when I was grabbed by plain clothes police when I was a little boy in Shamin, Canton, for throwing rocks at the foreign embassy children. And it was the general repressiveness of the Communist government at that time in China, which I see as a parallel is happening in this country right now. More about that later.

Also, my father was always a little paranoid because he was a small time crook and had been incarcerated at Angel Island for immigration interrogation when he came to this country. And there were threats against us when we were poor, some things I only know vaguely about. One incident I remember was that my father took me aside and told me where the revolver was in the house and told me to shoot whoever would try to break in at night. I was only about 14. That was when my father was possibly a partner at this house of prostitution, where he was employed as the cook at the restaurant, which was the cover for the whorehouse upstairs. I had to work there on the weekends at the restaurant when I was 14. The damage done me was that I couldn't sleep. But the biggest thing my father alluded to from time to time, was that he was a member of the Triad. The original Triad in China probably has its origin around 500 B.C., but in the recent 200 or so years, it has degenerated from an honor society to criminal organizations.

The reason all this is coming back now is probably because I have been "regressed" by Dr. Gallagher to childhood memories which have determined so much of my personality and manifestations of my mental illness. Now thanks to Dr. Jacobs, I am beginning to see what it is that I must do to unblock these inhibitions to write what was the facts and to interpret them in terms of my own life development.

There is much work to do. But this is the way I can relieve of my anger and humiliation and be a contributing member of society again. I came to this country, expecting to be friends with everyone. But within one year, a kid in school told me that I could never wash the "brown" off my hands, when we were in the lavatory. And then anyhow I was still elected the student president of my elementary school. Suddenly people who never talked to me walked me home that day. In China, you are supposed to be enemies for life with people who offended you, but in America, I realize that people can talk about differences. There are a lot of these cultural differences that I have to come to understand and to come to terms with. My father was a sorry and strange case. He hated white Americans and yet he smoked Marlboros, went duck hunting with a shotgun, and gambled at football pool. He became a fierce competitor in business, became a workaholic working 12 hours a day, all seven days a week, chained smoked, and drank gallons of coffee. He was very critical of less fortunate people, including his relatives. He taught himself to read the Wall Street Journal and to trade stocks with only an ESL education in English that he had learned as a night student when he worked at the naval shipyards as a young man in Oakland, CA. His greed for money as a substitute for all the things that he could not have been because he was an immigrant ultimately killed him at the age of 63. He died on the freeway on the way to pay his taxes of a heart attack.

It is a trick to find the time and money to write. You know that better than I do because I have been on SSI all this time since I was 28, except for brief periods when I was homeless.

Well, I hope we can help each other write and share our cultures.

Your friend,
Koon

And Dr. Laurence P. Jacobs told me that to have schizoaffective-bipolar mental illness, a patient could have inherited the genes or the propensity for it, or that *something happened to him.* He also told me that according to the textbooks he had read at Harvard Medical School, there's not supposed to be paranoia ideation associated with it, but in practice, it is often the case. I had written this next two poems about the Aberdeen experiences, one, *The Old House* and the other, *It Comes Through the Branches*; they both tell a little about the experiences and treatment I got while I was in Aberdeen after the development of my illness:

The Old House

Across dirt field,

Freights rumble through the evening pyre of burnt summer;

Light, off burnt grasses, raw honey, reflects

Into the anteroom through the blinds like X.J. Kennedy's

"Nude Descending Stairs,"

Rinds of light, yellow like bovine teeth,

like a manila envelope full of old receipts.

Also, milkfish, jade-green lights refract

Through the crabapple tree into the bedroom where I rest,

after swimming against the current for so many years in the pre-dawn

Light, no longer measuring myself against

The significant digits of the slide rule.

And the table lamp, incandescent, floods the room with yellow

Light at night on a yellow pad of paper. Here, was a birth

Of a thought which is not born is either ageless or will not live at all.

I began to trust the hand that guides a scalpel,

The hand that dress a wound.

The old house is

a kind asylum for Soviet dissidents

Who escape by turning themselves into spiders and traveling across the Tundra.

I lived here in Plato's Cave and dreamed of the Platonic heaven.

I studied the shadows. And Hank?

He is playing the Wednesday night Bingo.

It Comes Through the Branches

The crabapple tree, dense with leaves, wounded by age, its foliage
Fluttered open and closed.

Branches flutter, from this we know wind through gaps of leaves, like blanks

In my diary, where a subterranean form fluctuates through the years.

The forgetting function which forgets its argument, yet I remember the window pane

Where emerald light streamed in. The question may go like this of my life:

"And where were you on the day in question?"

The answer may be: "Sir, all my days are questions, but on that particular day,

I was leagues under the sea, of all things, naming, naming the things of this world:

A name is a handle on a cup, a tag on a suitcase.

I call Sam Sam and Harry Harry ---

Confucius said the first step to knowledge is calling

things by their correct names…"

The crabapples, stems, triangular leaves silhouette on the old house window pane

Like Sheffer strokes and other symbolic logic notation. The closure of the tree

Was the world. The knowing and the known once twirled in the bedroom like a

Flamenco dancer to the guitar of Carlos Montoya.:

Naming was a game on daffodils,

Ferns and clovers on the hills.

We live, we name, what we love, we love is name.

In one summer, the life span of insects.

In one afternoon, the tree flutters open, the tree flutters closed.

My ears, heavy with the music now. Think: Does the Oak care if you call it "Oak?"

Does the rose care if you call it "rose?" All language is naming. Sometimes

All you have to do is mention it: Say wind through the chimes and water on the Thames.

Say water rippling against the sand bar and fingers plucking the guitar…

Aberdeen was an isolated fauna and flora like the Bushmen's song of a distance,

Like the crucible in which we burnt things in high school chemistry,

Like creatures in a tide pool at Point Grenville.

This was Aberdeen, where I changed although my name remained the same.

***The Return* (two documents)**

Like criminals returning to the scene of the crime or Holocaust victims revisiting concentration camps I returned to Aberdeen to give a poetry reading, when my book of poems came out. I exhibit here two documents - one written in the Aberdeen newspaper when I returned to give a reading at the Aberdeen Public Library and the other written by a fellow classmate in high school.

Document 1

The Daily World Aberdeen newspaper, featured me on the front page of its Sunday paper on April 18, 1999 with this headline:

Poetic Justice: Koon Woon returns to Aberdeen

"In the pulse of saw mills I cut this logging town / Into board feet with my '55 Plymouth, with sawdust / Plenty to make ice cream cones."

--Koon Woon, "Aberdeen 1966, Or, Driving Around For a Poem," From "The Truth in Rented Rooms"

By Ryan Teague Beckwith

Daily World Writer

"To Koon Woon, life is a series of rented rooms. Some - like the village he was born near Canton in China or the three-bedroom house on Oak Street in Aberdeen that he moved into at age12 - are literal. 'Everybody in a sense is living in a rented room," he said in a phone interview last week, 'In a more profound way, we are all renting time on Earth.'

"Now 50 and living in an apartment in Seattle's International District, Woon has published 'The Truth in Rented Rooms,' his first book of poetry and a reflection of his transcendental philosophy.

Already, the 112-page book has garnered praise from *The Village Voice* and fame San Francisco beat poet Lawrence Ferlinghetti among others. On Thursday, he will face an altogether more personal audience: his former hometown.

"When Woon reads from his poems at the Aberdeen Timberland Library Thursday, the crowd will likely include a number of old friends who remember the mop-haired young boy who studied English after school and built crystal radios out of toilet paper tubes and copper wires in his spare time.

Back them, those who knew him - and Woon himself - though he would grow up to become a scientist or maybe an engineer.

" ' I always thought he could do whatever he wanted,' said Aberdeen Deputy Police Chief Dave Timmons, who went to school with Woon.

"Woon spoke no English when he immigrated to America to be with his parents, Bill and Kim, who then owned the Hong Kong Café on Simpson Avenue. He first encountered poetry in a high school class that touched on Walt

Whitman's 'Leaves of Grass.' Though he like 'the grandeur and voice' of the poems, Woon said he didn't think much of it at the time.

"Instead, he started studying math and science in night classes at Grays Harbor College while still in high school. By the time he graduated in 1968, he was already a sophomore in college. He transferred to the University of Washington to continue studying electrical engineering but 'something happened.'

" ' I was unable to concentrate,' he said. 'I dropped out of school and drifted around for a few years, taking some classes at the University of Oregon and in San Francisco. I drifted on and off.'

"In the mid 1980's, Woon was diagnosed with bipolar manic depression and hospitalized in St. Francis Memorial Hospital in San Francisco for three months. He turned to poetry as a form of therapy, writing about growing up in Canton and moving to America. A number of pieces that he groups together as 'The Aberdeen Poems' about his days here and published in a Seattle magazine.

"The poems are not exactly paeans to the joys of Aberdeen. Woon writes about the loneliness and isolation he felt as a Chinese-American in a town of Scandinavians and Croatian immigrants, writing in one that 'The doctors in the antiseptic Becker Building can't take away/This and other pains of a small town' and in another about 'Agent orange sky.'

"Not long after those poems were published, Woon had some of work accepted into a competition at the Bumbershoot arts festival in Seattle. He went on to study under Nelson Bentley at the University of Washington's acclaimed writing program and has since had poems accepted in about 30 magazines.

"Last year, a friend encouraged him to send a group of his poems o different publishers. The first publisher rejected him because they don't accept original work, but the second company he contacted – Kaya Publishing of New York – agreed on an initial run of 1,000 copies.

" ' It made me feel vindicated,' Woon said. 'It made me feel that I was onto something, feeling something that other people felt.'"

The reading at the Aberdeen public library did take place, and a fellow classmate, Mike Maki, came to the reading, which was mainly attended by older ladies and friends of the library. Mike Maki was in both my creative writing class and Senior Honors English class in Aberdeen High School and this was what he had read to introduce at the library:

Document 2

"Welcome back, Koon Woon 4-20-1999

And so Koon Woon, it's you!
Back on the Harbor after all these seasons.
I've often wondered where you'd gone.

I remember in golden spring light
our high school days
At the beginning and end of an era.
When the Anglo-Saxon innocence of Aberdeen,
Washington and Weatherwax High
Gave way simultaneously to acute awareness
of the war in Asia,
And the exuberant expansion of consciousness
everywhere
Our class rushed and fell into chaos
of a culture changing in most every way.

And you, Koon, one of our handful of
minority students,

arriving in Aberdeen from distant China
with your family
I remember your shy but eager enthusiasm
and your voracious appetite for knowledge

I remember being there with you
in Miss Gwin's honors English class.
That odd mix of briefcase-toting geeks,
earnest overachievers, and guys like me,
Pulling A's in school by day, and Chevy
engines at night.
Wild weekends of Rainier Draft beer
Cruising and carousing, while you studied
in your apron at a tooth in the back
of your family's restaurant.

Of course you recall sweetly senile,
mumbling Miss Gwin
who lived for her annual pilgrimage with
her spinster friends to Ashland, Oregon's
Shakespeare Festival.

Who confused the names of the sons
with their fathers,
whom she had taught in the same
classroom a generation before.
But that wasn't your problem, a new-
comer dedicated to mastering English,
and doing so with varsity proficiency.

Surely you remember our fellow students,
The eggheads and the future elite
The smart-asses and the soc's, the
iconoclasts and the quiet studious ones
All bound for some kind of glory,
insulated from the jungle destiny of
our less fortunate classmates.
Full of humor and hope,
In a small city near the sea.

And you, Koon Woon, with your briefcase
and cow-lick
Reading Thomas Mann and Herman Hesse,

and god knows what else.
Asking philosophical questions in your
Chinese accent
That sometimes caught us all off guard
And made us see with new eyes,
and question our youthful assumptions.

There was John Imme, the irreverent son
of minister, a trickster by nature.
And Craig Wickland, our charismatic class
president with a wicked sense of humor.
Baffling Miss Gwin with double entendre
and whispered asides.
Tom Osheroff, the 'brain,' whose mother
waited for him outside "Y' dances with the
motor running, waiting impatiently
to return him home to study, while he
secretly longed to be a teenager.
And Gail Waara, Carol Sundquist, and
all the rest of the adolescent intelligentsia.
We were all somewhat in awe of you,

Koon,

With your questioning mind and serious

cheerfulness.

There was Miss Freelin, the creative

writing teacher barely older than we

were.

Who encouraged us to look deeply into

life and then find words to express

our feelings.

It all made sense to me one day a

couple of years later, when I ran

into her and her boyfriend on the

Ave, and she smiled and winked

approvingly at the person I was

becoming, and we saw each other as peers.

Mr. Shillinger taught us journalism and

how to produce the Ocean Breeze school

newspaper.

He gave me copies of the L.A. Free Press,

The Helix, and the Berkeley Barb,
and encouraged us to be free thinkers.

Your and I met again from time to
time in passing at the University of
Washington,
It's kaleidoscopic campus blazing in
late 1960's,
Our hair longer, our eyes more open,
a fire in our hearts.
You were hanging out with Chinese
professors and foreign grad students,
Taking acid and talking late into the
night about physics and metaphysics,
and the meaning of life.

I wish you could have joined our crowd
sometimes,
A the rope swing under the Ravenna bridge,
Where we talked of love and mysticism
and radical social change and

a hopeful future beyond war and
racism;
Where we listened in psychedelic revelry
to the spring flowers blooming, and
to the secret language of the birds,
And played soulful music to accompany
one impending peaceful revolution.

I wish you could have joined me on
the hiking trails of the Olympics.
We would have read from the poetry
of Gary Snyder and the prose of
John Muir,
And made up poems for each other, to
celebrate the mountains' moment.
And drunk in the beauty and mystery
of my native land.
But our paths parted, and I lost
all track of you.

Then somewhere I heard you were

dead, Koon.
And I was sad that our sketchy
conversation, so full of potential and
implicit agreement
Could not continue.
Perhaps, they said, it was like Osheroff,
and you were dead by your own
overachieving but empty, lonely hand.
Slain by a hidden grief and a
deep uncertainty.

But here you are,
Bringing words engraved from your
life experiences.
A trail of footprints upon the
wooden fiber.
Where did you go, Koon?
How has it been?
Tell us of crossing the tenuous bridge
between heart an mind and tongue
and emigrant hand.

And welcome back!"

How I became a poet

When I lived at 416 ½ in Seattle Chinatown I lived in #317. I was being ridiculed and bullied in the U-District and I could ill-afford to eat when my room on 16th NE was $170 a month while my SSI was only $300 a month. I called my mother when I have paranoia and she would yank the phone from its jack. She finally told her younger brother Chay who lived in Chinatown to find a room for me where he lived, and that was at 416 ½. The room was a tenement but it had one redeeming value – it had a small table that I can place a typewriter on. The rent was $60 a month. I moved in.

Allen Hikida, my former teacher at Seattle Central Community College told me that maybe I should take a workshop from Nelson Bentley at the UW. Hikida had done a Master's thesis under Bentley's supervision. I went to Padelford Hall on the UW campus where the English Department was but Nelson Bentley (NB) was never in his office so it seemed. I got impatient and I called his home.

"Have you done much of this poetry stuff?" He asked.

"Yes, even including some that you had rejected, " I fibbed. And so he let me come to the evening workshop, which unofficially was open to anyone who was a current student or a former student of the UW. I was not even in English. That tells you his generosity and kindness. I felt so grateful I would come a half an hour early and helped him arranged the chairs in two concentric circles for his class which was attended from anywhere from 20 to 40 students twice a week two hours per evening.

And so I wrote this poem celebrating the memory of Nelson Bentley:

adapted from the Chinese by

Koon Woon

NB* as Gungfu Master

When I first arrived at the workshed as an itinerant boxer I told
NB I wanted to learn Gungfu. He said fine if you can parry my
punch and he threw a roundhouse punch to my ear. But he was so
slow and obvious that I was able to utter onomatopoeia before
he could land the blow. I said NB teach me the real stuff. I
will he said if you can stop a kick to the shin and watch out
for metaphors at the same time. I realized then that Gungfu is
deadly stuff especially when he recited RMi
lhouseN as America's
anti-self as he kicked. I said ok NB what do I have to do? NB
said I will teach you if you carry my calf everyday as you do
your chores, carry it everywhere you go. I saw that it was a
small calf and myself being a robust man I said ok that's easy.
And so I carried the calf in my arms everyday from the workshed
to the river to the fields, learning gradually the nifty shortcuts
in my daily rounds. At the end of each year I ask NB if I am
ready to learn Gungfu now. He always says wait until the calf
is a little bit bigger. After 10 years I thought I am wasting my
time scooping up calf dung for the past 10 years and so I said
to NB, who was now venerable and who carries a batch of pencil
stubs and a bundle of small notebooks which grew in size as my
calf did. Are you ready to teach me Gungfu? He said how much
did the calf weigh when you first came to the workshed? I said
about
100 catties. He said you carried it? I said yes. And he said
for the last 10 years you have been carrying the calf everyday

as you jumped over fences and ditches have you not? I said yes. How much does the calf weigh now? About 1,000 catties, I answered.
When you first came you could carry 100 catties but now you can Carry 1,000 catties and jump over ditches and streams can you not? I said yes. How high and how far can you jump if you weren't carrying the cow? I began to see his point. I bowed. NB then said I have never taught Gungfu. I have taught something else.
I bowed again and he took back his cow.

*NB = Nelson Bentley, English Professor at the UW Seattle

(Published circa 1988 by the Bellowing Ark Press in *Nelson Bentley Memoriam)*

Then an old friend, Martin Ingerson, playwright and poet, adept this poem to a short play, "Kan Fa (Perspectives):"

KAN FA (PERSPECTIVE)

CHARACTERS

Professor Whang — noted teacher

Mrs Whang — his wife

Young Student

SCENE: Seattle Chinatown — International District

(Professor Whang, Wife and Student stand near Whang's top floor

apartment picture window.)

STUDENT Professor Whang, I've left my parents in Sacramento

as an artist to learn perspective. I've heard that you are a master

in the seldom mentioned Song Dynasty technique of horizons,

called "Kan Fa".

PROF WHANG Kan Fa! Ah! Very obscure.

STUDENT Yes. That's why I've come to Seattle, to your budget condo

in Uwajamaya Village. I wish to learn Kan Fa.

PROF WHANG Fine. If you can name and date first Renaissance Italian

practitioner, while standing on left foot.

STUDENT *(standing on left foot)* Filippo Brunelleschi. 1377 to 1446.

Come on, Professor; teach me the real stuff.

PROF WHANG Ah! Look to point west between two huge Arenas

called "Safeco" and "Century Link" Fields. What point to you see?

STUDENT The vanishing point.

PROF WHANG Wrong! It's the point where the ticket prices become

too expensive to afford. The Vanishing Point is where players testify

on steroid use.

STUDENT This is deadly stuff. *(bowing)* Please teach me.

PROF WHANG I will teach you if you walk my dog each day

to her favorite chestnut tree in Kobe Terrace Park … and other chores.

STUDENT Your dog is a Lhasa Apso. Can I carry her on rainy days?

PROF WHANG I said "walk". And other chores.

STUDENT *(after pause)* Okay.

PROF WHANG *(aside to Wife)* The boy will work well.

MRS WHANG Get him to take out the laundry.

(One year later)

STUDENT Professor, I've walked your dog to Kobe Park for a year.

Now am I ready for Kan Fa?

PROF WHANG Wait until the dog gets bigger.

MRS WHANG Get him to pick up this week's Uwajamaya Bargain Flyer.

(Five years later)

STUDENT Professor Whang, I've taken your dog five years to pee

at her favorite Chestnut tree and she hasn't grown any bigger.

Lhasa Apsos don't grow. Is it time to teach me Kan Fa?

PROF WHANG Ah! You have seen now that it's not the dog,

but the tree that draws you. Trees are Time's Kan Fa. Their

bare limbs are a Fourth Dimension Map. Keep observing.

MRS WHANG Tell him to collect the chestnuts this winter.

(Ten years later)

STUDENT Professor, I've been collecting chestnuts for five years

and scooping up dog poop for ten years and now I think I'm

wasting my time. Are you gong to teach me?

PROF WHANG Ah! Today we go to tree in Kobe Terrace.

I will teach you "shortcut"?

STUDENT *(amazed)* A shortcut? I've walked there ten years!

PROF WHANG Shortcut in eyes! Not feet.

STUDENT Binocular disparity?

PROF WHANG Shortcut in perception! Point of view. One slip

and you learn nothing. Do you understand me?

STUDENT Sure.

MRS WHANG *(aside to Whang)* You're not going to teach him!

If he thinks he's learned Kan Fa, he'll leave us!

PROF WHANG *(aside to Wife)* Relax, Bunnycheeks. I have things

under control.

(Short time later. Near Chestnut tree in Kobe Terrace Park.)

PROF WHANG Now, young man, as you gaze out over Elliott Bay

toward the majestic Olympic Mountain, name the root of "perception".

STUDENT Uh … ocular discernment?

PROF WHANG Wrong! Discipline! Discipline and obedience fix the root-

in-the-eyes, the perspective, the vanishing point. You must do exactly

everything I say.

STUDENT Okay.

PROF WHANG Good. Climb up tree to top branch. Keep gaze fixed

on mountains. Go.

(Student climbs up the tree and looks at Olympic Mountains.

Sound of small dog barking.)

MRS WHANG *(to Whang)* Do you know what you're doing? Fool!

He'll leave!

PROF WHANG Relax, Honeybunch.

(shouting up to Student) Young man, carefully grab top branch

with both hands!! Now hang from branch with hands!!

(Student hangs from branch.) Young man, let go with left hand!!

(Student hangs by right hand.) Now let go with right hand!!

MRS WHANG *(smugly)* He won't do it.

PROF WHANG We will see.

(Student lets go of right hand, but instead of falling;

he rises and floats off over Safeco Field and Elliot Bay

toward Mount Olympus among blue Olympic peaks

[atmospheric perspective].)

PROF WHANG He floats over Safeco Field to Olympics, to the blue

mountains, to China

MRS WHANG Stupid! He's gone!

PROF WHANG *(smiling)* He was going anyway.

(Sound of dog barking fades quickly. Dim out.)

Note: on black box stages or in a theatre without a fly gallery

the Student on a platform upstage simply mimes the tree climbing,

hanging on branch, and floating off.

Martin Ingerson

Seattle

I don't today, at age sixty-six, and believe anything much anymore. I just want to tell the reader that I have suffered two-thirds of my life with schizoaffective mental illness, and my village years, though hard and unforgiving, was what enabled me to survive my prolonged illness. And it is not only the mental illness, it is also how other people misunderstand and are sometimes cruel to you if you are different. Yes, I would fit the bill in today's culture of "political correctness." I am "Asian, immigrant, and disabled," and elderly now and low-income. This qualifies me to Medicaid, SSI, and low-income public housing and an allotment of food stamps. I am telling you that I live like a King in the Middle Ages and comparing my early life in the village, I would have lived like an emperor in China's long illustrious but also sad history.

Betty:

One day in August 1996, yes, it was the fifth of August I received a long distance call from Wisconsin and the inquirer asked me, "Are you the editor of Chrysanthemum?"

I said yes but I was not publishing my small zine at the time and I said I was willing to look at her work. And so she sent me a short story. Upon receiving it in a hypomanic mood, I wrote back, "This story is so horrible, please don't send me any more work for five years!"

She, instead of getting angry, Betty thought it was honest and hilarious. And so she called me frequently even as I tried to block the calls, but I couldn't block them, according to the operator, because they are interstate calls.

Finally I acquiesced and talked with her and found out she is a retired librarian. She then asked me whether I wrote poetry. I told her that I did. She then asked me to send a batch of them to her to look at. I sent twenty poems.

This started the avalanche. She immediately acted as my "agent" in sending my work to publishers. The first place we send the poems to was the University of Hawaii and they wrote back immediately that they do not publish original poems but only translations from Asia. Betty then send the poems to Kaya Press , which was at New York at the time. Julie Koo and Sunyoung Lee were the managing editor and literary editor at the time. They wrote back that they would seriously consider it. Two months later, they accepted my book.

Perhaps the human elements of this book's reach is worth more than any of the craft of the poems themselves.

The long and short of this is the birth of the book The Truth in Rented Rooms, which received unexpected acceptance, which led to my second book with Kaya, Water Chasing Water.

This gave me the confidence I needed to return to school to finish my BA degree at Antioch University Seattle and onto graduate school at Fort Hays State University.

I thus gained personal friendships and publishing success.

The Beacon Hill Canto

I.

I will pay for the breeze, brief as it is,
rippling across the shroud of green leaves
shooting above the ravine, in this sun-flecked
Beacon Hill neighborhood,
where life is idle,
and Dylan Thomas would pronounce it good.

Rain or shine, here it boasts of a solitary café:
(As Prospero's Island)
[The Station],
as in a station of the metro,
"the apparitions of these faces in a crowd"
(a small intimate crowd it is),
"petals on a wet, black, bough."

And would it have been worth it,
after tea, coffee, or cocoa,
marshmallow or orange marmalade
that will take you to another level of satisfaction?
I begin my morning walk
as my mood and the street propel me
past houses with eaves and green paint,
past shrubs patiently manicured and variegated roses that grace
communal pledges.
We are here to rescue each other from sad days
Like a body that catches a body coming
Through the rye
while gardeners master the flowers and
measure without malice and weigh without hate.

II.

Let us cross Beacon Hill Avenue to the Red Apple,
A grocery like Prospero's Island in the hunger sea
You can take your sums from the Wells Fargo ATM,
go inside the store and give your eyes a feast,
and remember to purchase a book of stamps,
for letters to connect with Texas and Tennessee.
Let's now continue past the branch library,
but we will not linger now, for there is time,
time for you and time for me,
time for the hope of the woman,
even though our principles have been hijacked
by the congressional corporations.
O Ezra Pound, where are you now?
Thou were the CEO of Modernist Poetry.
Why did you take up residence at Saint Elizabeth?
Asylum for the insane?
Oh well we won't go see the Muse,
and even without a single glimpse of the Muse,
the walk must go on; we shall go on.

III.

Inside his mind was the Muse.
And she moves on, as the river;
as the water, she moves on.
Stones will not impede her.
Shameless she provides,
in the estuary,
when birds rest there from their flight.

IV.

That was another time.
He was on an island most of his days,
protected from unprivileged eyes.

V.

And she was in the open.
She called for the sky,
there came the sky.
And she wanted rain.
She received rain and became fertile again.

VI.

The walk resumes past the bicycle shop
on Beacon Hill Avenue,
I am of this time and of this place.
A bicycle won't transform into a unicycle.
The streets parade by with their designations
Horton, Hinds, and Spokane at the Fire Station.
And voices are heard, songs sung, the roses bloom,
and so don't cry, little ones with little eyes.
Sometimes we are silent but today we are multilingual,

VII.

De la sierra, morena
Cielito lindo vienen bajando
Un par de ojitos negros
Cielito lindo de contrabando

Ay, ay, ay, ay, canta y no llores
Porque cantando se alegran
Cielito lindo los corazones

VIII.

So please order a drink

and I do not get a cut, and
price is right.
We do not object.
We do not object to its price.

Jin tien wo men cher fan
Wo men do shih cher fan

"In the café the women come and go,
talking of Michaelangelo."

And at the Station of the Metro
"The many faces of the crowd
"Petals on a wet, black bough."

Journal

Here's my own "Creation Myth"

In the beginning out of the Void and Chaos there was only one Being, who called himself God. He was a lonely guy because although he had the means to slow, stop, or to speed up time, to travel from one dimension to another, to create galaxies and parallel universes as easily as you and I could say "Pie" he had no one to appreciate his powers and his ken. He hadn't even contemplated the idea of a Dog yet, which was merely the spelling of his name backwards. But one day, as he was traveling through deep space, through a "worm hole" created by a massive dying star, which was creating a black hole, he noticed that he was getting warmer and warmer as his infinite being was being sucked into the black hole. An incredible insight came to him from this darkness. He contemplated a department store called Sears, Roebuck, and Company; he further contemplated all the things that he could create for this variety store. He thought of washers and dryers, television sets, computers, shoes, hats, winter mittens, and even chain saws. He thought even of home improvement kits but there was no complex organism such as Himself that could appreciate what he was capable of. His loneliness only deepened until he thought of an entity called "Man." [The reader is advised to read the word "man" as a generic term for man, woman, boy, or girl] So, he invented dough, the kind that you make cake and donuts out of and not the slang for money. He fashioned the dough into little figures of men, women, and children. He put them into the oven which he had previously invented. But since he hadn't invented a timer and a thermometer yet, he had to estimate how much time to cook each batch of tiny dough figurines of the people he had fashioned. So, he put the first batch into the oven, but he took them out too soon. They came out as the "white" people. So, he told himself that the second batch has to stay a little longer in the oven. But he waited a little too long, and so the second batch came out too well done and so they were the "black" people. And so to remedy the situation, He put in the third batch and took it out timing it carefully. And so they came out just right. He called these the Asian people [a bit of reverse racism here].

And so He created people. Even though the people became highly knowledgeable and civilized after a few million years or so, they kind of forgotten about Him, and so He invented Immaculate Conception and created a Son of his own. He called it Godson. Some people wanted him to call his Son by the names of Jesus, Mohammed, Buddha, or whatever, but since God is God and there is no way of telling him what to do, Godson became part of the vocabulary and reality. So, this was the Original Story. Then the people created Hollywood. After that, nobody knows the truth anymore (end).

FRANK CHIN INTERVIEWS KOON WOON

SEPTEMBER 5, 2007

KOON WOON (1949-)

For some reason he's dropped his family surname Locke (Horse with a woman on top of a mouth) from his name Gok in Cantonese or Kuo (nation) in Mandarin. Kuan (Lum on the left. Don't know meaning). Locke Gok Kuan born in the village of Nom On became Koon Woon when he came into the United States by plane in 1960.

CHIN: OK this is once again. It's uh August...Septempber. September what?

KOON WOON: 5th.

CHIN: September 5th...

K: 2007. Wednesday, at the Panama Coffee Tea...Coffee or Tea House...

C: Right.

K: 605

C: ...and a half...

K: 605 1/2

K: South Main Street...

C: in Seattle. A little overcast. With Koon Woon and Frank Chin. Uhhh. Well, let's start at the beginning. With your name. So, I see the "mah"

K: Lok. Kok

C: Yeah.

K: No, I mean...I think it's Lawk.

C: Lawk tawk is a camel. And lawk is a part of a camel?

K: Gradations of a camel, or a white horse with a black mane.

C: Gawk, the nation or country. And Koon (kuen).

K: (cellphone gives an orchestra. Kooon answers) Hi Betty. ... We're in the middle of an interview, Betty. ... Okay.

C: So...Eh! So...you learned to write before you went to school.

K: No, actually I learned to...I went to grade school in China for five years. So I learned it there. I learned ahh...what I did learn,

I learned how to play poker before I went to school.
I became the best poker player in my village. And I became the poker player in my grade school.

But the thing I was best at was mathematics. I was the best student in mathematics in my gradeschool in China. The best in uh Canton, and the best in Hong Kong, in the private school I went to.

And when I came to the United States, I was the 2nd best in the high school. They found my math was so good that the uh MIT asked me to join them a year early out of high school.

Today...Unfortunately I had a genetic defect which caused mmental illness in my twenties. And I've been on medication ever since. My late twenties. So that chapter of my just sort of evaporated.

C: Explain how your uncle taught you to write "Liao"

K: Well actually I went to my...The grade school I went to was in my grandmother's village. My maternal grandmother's village. And one of clansman, the teacher that taught to write...to remember how to write the last name "Liao" He says...He says, "One point. One horizontal stroke. One slant to the left. Two half moons. One person. And three half persons." So if you follow that instruction in Chinese you would have the character "Liao"which is just a family surname. There's no other indication in the dictionary having any other kind of meaning.

C: What was your village name?

K: Nam On. Which means "South Peace."

C: Where was the village in relation to Kuangzho?

K: Okay. The village is in the Sirbo district of Toishan County. Toishan County is about 100 miles southwest of Kuangchow, which used to be Canton. Called Canton.

C: What was the climate there like?

K: It's semi tropical. And we go things with you get think...the tip of a... you know the bottom part of this country...part of Mexico...semi-tropical. We have lot of... it's hot and humid. And it's uhh we get monsoons in May an' which literally floods the whole villages. There be water everywhere. You can't see land at all. The wells would be flooded. The pond would be flooded. The road would be flooded. The rivers would be flooded. So you can't see where you're going. Then theoretically you could catch a fish outside your own house...with a...with a net. The all the rivers have overflowed. So when the monsoon recedes the water's trapped in the rice paddies. The rice paddies have dikes in them.

C: Right.

K: So some of the fish gets trapped in the rice paddies. So when the you and so when the sun comes out, you know, when the weather gets hot, the fish will swim up near the surface groggy headed, so you just go to with a bucket and pickemup, and bring your bucket. That's your biggest harvest of fish a year.

C: Monsoon season's what?

K: About May. Chinese calendar May.

C: And the paddy...

K: The water recedes from the monsoon and some of the water be trapped in the rice paddies. And so he can plant rice seedlings in the mud.

C: And other things in the village?

K: We well...green gardens, we have dry gardens, and we grew seasonal vegetables. We grew bok choy, lettuce, winter melon, peas and corn things like that. Then we grow dry...in the dry garden we grow yams and peanuts and things like that.

C: Would there be different levels?

K: Terrace? No. No. No. We would put the gardens right next to the village pond. So we could dip the sprinkler in the village pond and sprinkle water in the garden, and later the water would flow right into the village pond. And so I did that twice a day, for my grandmother, uh... watered her plants.

C: Was there a brick wall around your village?

K: On one side of it, there's a brick wall, but not, I mean there's no doors or anything. Just a brick wall. The wall. The next village. So, it demarcated the next village. But parts of the village is open, you know. Completely open.

C: And you said the Manchus had uhhhh

K: Oh, yeah. We were talking about the uhhh. The manchus conquered China, but uhh where we were, the southern coast revolted. Some of the people driven to Formosa, what was still called Formosa. Or Taiwan these days. So the...the Manchus are afraid that these people will come back and revolt again. So they import a lot of northerners, to southern China. And they're they're a different tribe of people, they're much taller. They're called the Hakka. That's what they're called. Hakka.

So the uhh constant struggle between the Hakka and the local people....in the late...in the early 1800's is sort of a war between the Hakka and indigional people. And so a lot of people...the salmon decided...a lot of people from my area of China emigrated to the United States. And so that's why you find so many Toisahnese in these country. Original founders of this country were Toisahnese.

C: So, you were born in China.

K: Yes.

C: And you came over...

K: 1960.

C: And you were how old?

K: I was almost 12. I was 11 in ten months....eight months or something...I came on Halloween night, in China. And I came to the United States, it was still Halloween night, although it was twelve hours later, cuz of the time differential, so I gained a day.

C: Do you remember a story of how people were made?

K: Yes. How people were made. That's uhh sort of like a uhh...I don't remember, but my mother told me in this country...the people told me in the village, but the god that made people, you know, I guess he was lonely, so he made people out of dough, so he put'em in the oven to bake'em to make'em come alive. The first batch he put in, he took'em out too soon. So they're white people. So, the second batch he said I gotta leave a little longer. So he took'em out, they became the black people. The third batch he put in, he time it just right, it came out that they're Asian people. Heh Heh. So that's reverse racism.

C: Did you come directly from the village to America or were there steps in between?

K: There were steps in between. The immigration was very stringent at that time, because in the United States and China they're very hostile relationship. So we had to...even back in the village when I was a little boy nine years old, we were, you know, doing the paperwork to get out of China. So like then we have to go to Canton, the City Kuangchow, for two years to continue the paperwork there. I lived in Canton for two years. The we finally was able to make it out to Hong Kong. We waited ten months in Hong Kong before allowed to leave the country come to the United States.

C: What were conditions like in Kwangzhao?

K: Kwangchow was a Mao Tse-tung's Five Year Great Leap Forward plan. He wanted to quickly industrialize China, because at that time the United States were flying B-2 (Sic) bombers or...with nuclear weapons over China. You don't have to believe me, you can ask other people who actually flew those planes. I have a guy a editorial....a editor of the HASMET Magazine in New York, upstate New York, he told me, that he flew one of those planes. B-52's whatever they were called, you know, over North Korea and China. With lethal weapons on them.

C: Wow!

K: Uh yeah. We uh the newspaper announce everday "The US has violated our airspace for the 155th time! When are we going to do something about it?"

(HUGE LAUGHTER)

Course, they couldn't do anything about it, so Mao Tse-tung wanted to quickly industrialize China and build a modern army. So he got all the people from the villages to go to the cities to take on the industry...unit. In the... So as a consequence in the not many people were farming the land and they were also hit with a -bike- bad famine day. So a lot of people starve to death. The food was rationed, and we had to stand in line. We were issued food rations. Besides paying for the food. I had to stand in line for my grandmother's food. Couple hours in the morning just to buy food.

C: And what would the food be?

K: Well, you were rationed, right? Four ounces of meat a week, or something. (Train horns) And you would just get rice. And the you know that's bo(?) a lot. But you couldn't very much, you know.

C: Was the rice in Guangzhao as good as the rice in the village?

K: Well. I suppose that's where it came from. It's just as good. But thing is, you know what the congee is right?

C: Yes.

K: Those are the years we ate a lot of congee.. So you'd be eating essentially water. To make the water...the rice go a long way, you just make congee.

C: So, you were in Guangzhao two years?

K: Two years. Yes. Some of the time was okay. I mean, there was food one year. But one year was rationed. Yeah.

CHIN: How did you spend your time.

K: Well, school and at the uh...We had the, you know, China was in the socialist era, at that time, so, okay, we had uh..we had to like a...we had to work for the school. We had to volunteer. We had to help campaigns and like I myself and a bunch of other boys we issued tickets with the people spit on the street. We went out and to make fly swatters. We killed flies ...on the street. And we helped the uhh drain, you know, standing water. We were janitors for the school. We work half a day for the school, shelling peanuts or scraping bottle caps and... do various things like that, and the uh. But, I remember one thing, I was kept after school to do math. I said, you know, I says, I don't seem to have trouble with math. That I would keep... They keep me after school with a couple of kids. Cuz I was exceedingly good in math, where they were teaching me complex fractions and things like that...so...So when I got to this country, I you know, they put me in the third grade, and say, you know, I didn't have to think. You know, I was still...They were still learning the multiplication table I learned in the first grade in China.

C: How large were the classes in China?

K: In the village we had fifty...We just...all the villages we just have one school. All the villages we just have one school, the several villages, so maybe a coupe hundred people in the whole school. So the fifth grade, that would be about, I know, about thirty or forty people a...a room.

In the Kwangchow...the students..we had about, um maybe about twenty thirty people in the classroom. Yeah.

C: Were the teachers women teachers or men teachers?

K: Both women and men. Yeah.

C: What was the etiquette in the classroom?

K: Uh Well, uh...in...in... In Kuangchow...In... In the village it was kind of a, you know casual. In Kwangchow it was very strict. We had to sit with our hands behind our back. We could not speak, and we could not, you know, pass notes. And when you want to speak, in the class, you have to raise your hand. You get recognized by the teacher, and you have to stand up. And you have to say what you want to say, as quickly and as succinctly as possible.

And as soon as you say, you have to sit down. And the teacher will make an account of what you say, and then nobody else can speak in response to what you say, unless they're recognized by the teacher.

C: Hmmm!

K: However! After school, then you go ...you split into study groups, and you quiz each other. What you learned of... uk....during the day.

C: Hmmm!

K: And the teacher would not, you know, would not correct you, or anything like that. So, it was a good learning experience. But the reason we, you know, we had this...raise our hand is to learn discipline, is to learn to pay attention.

C: So these groups...did you find yourself becoming a teacher of math?

K: Well. Actually, we uh...Actually, we...we didn't have a study groups in math.

C: Umm.

K: Because as Uh. Yeah. We did have study groups like uh, you know, "literature"

C: Mmmm!

K: or umm "History" or something like that. ...was open to interpretation.

C: Umm hmmm.

KOON: Math is, you know, either you got it right, you got it wrong.

C: Right.

K: So, you don't argue with somebody about it. You know?

C: You talked about Monkey.

K: Yes.

C: Yeah. Uh, Uhh. When did you encounter Monkey?

K: I believe I read the JOURNEY TO THE WEST. Three sets of books, right? In the Canton Public Library. It was between 9 and 11. In Canton. I was too young to check books out at the library, so I had to go to library to read it every day. It's a real fascinating book, you know, cuz it's all about fantasy and it's all about supernatural, well you know, tales. So that was just like...Children like comic books. The kids in this country.

CHIN: SAI YOW GAY has another meaning?

KOON: It sounds to me in Toishanese as Say Yow Gay. Say means, you know the number four. Well, West (say) sounds like the number four. Which means "Death" in Chinese.
The Tibetan Book of the Dead, is like that...the journey of the Dead. Cuz sounds to me in my own mind, sounds like...Journey of the Dead. Which to me in Buddhism, you know like uh, Buddhism, the whole idea of Buddhism is to reach enlightenment, you know, after suffering becuz we have suffered because of the human body.

The Human body is just like a corpse. You carry it around, you know, it's a burden of a body. You carry it around like a corpse.

We feed it, you know. Especially those indulgent people, you know, they eat all those fatty food, drink a lot of whiskey, smoke a lot cigarettes, all those vices, you know.

C: Everything I do.

When we met you were living across the street at the International Terrace.

KOON: Yes.

CHIN: And now you've been moved out.

KOON: I moved out. Yes. I moved out.

CHIN: What was behind that?

KOON: Well. Okay. I got a notice, one day. Says that the uh from the property manager, she said, "I got the notice on you. You're being investigated for fraud and perjury."

C: Hmm!

KOON: And then, uh, "You have 3 days to bring us your financial records." So, I thought that was very strange, that the uh, that I had only three days to gather up my things to uuh for a, you know, from a uh fraud investigation.

C: Right.

K: And then uh..I didn't show up because uh uh because I was so upset, I was meditating to my computer. My computer has a meditation website that sounds of medidating and I fell asleep at the hour I was supposed go down to the office, in the building to do the interview.

And they didn't call my room. They didn't call my phone number. And they didn't come to my door, to knock on my door, to get me down there. So, I missed the meeting.

So, they send me another letter. This time they gave me a date, you know, to come down. It was this time was a more "Notice." But still I had no idea of what they were looking for. So, so I considered that a fishing expedition. Okay? The uh ...You know. The...Legally you call "fishing expedition." Where you're just trying to gather information on somebody. Hopefully you find something derogatory or detrimental to that person.

So, the uh. So I brought all my financial records. And they said, you know, uh, "It seems like you have extra money. That you're not reporting."

So, I said, "Well, you know, as you can see, these are debts. These are credit card debts. These are student loans. And none of this would be considered income."

And they said, "Well, you have a trust. Don't you?"

I said, "Yes, I...here's the paper to the trust. And then uh...And then later on, they says, "How come you didn't report your trust?"

I said, "I report my trust every year that they income review."

And that they said, "We don't have any record of it."

I said, "Now look at the logic of the situation. It does not mean that I burglarized you place and removed all the records, right? It could mean that you removed all the records. It could mean that you never put the records there. Okay? Just because you don't have the records, doesn't mean that I didn't give you the records. Okay?"

So, they said they have no records. However! Uh. My room was burglarized, and the checks to my trust were stolen. So, I had to change the account to my trust. And then they uh...At the bank. They have records of it at the bank. And then they come back to me later, subsequent time, Seattle

Housing they says to me, says, "How come you changed your trust account?"

Now how would they know I changed it unless they had the old account and new account?

Chin: Mmm!

KOON: So they have records of my trust.

CHIN: Right.

KOON: They. So they…they uh you know they made a mistake that they contradicted themselves.

CHIN: Right.

KOON: So they do have proof. They do have records of my trust. So.

CHIN: Who runs the…

KOON: The property managers that I was dealing with, her name is Pamela Rohrbeck. And she is charge of several sites, besides this one.

CHIN: For…

KOON: Seattle Housing Authority, which is now just managing the property for a private owner. Because the building has been privatized. The Seattle Housing Authority is part of…HUD…I believe. And then uh the jurisdiction of HUD, which is a federal agency, although the HUD Director, I understand is appointed by the mayor. But once appointed by the mayor he no longer answers to HUD….I mean, to the mayor, he answers to HUD which is directly controlled by the White House. Ultimately.

CHIN: Um! And HUD can sell the building or convert it to condos or do anything they want?

KOON: Uh! Let's see. Now the uh. Well the...Actually it's owned by a private owner. The private owner, if they have approval by HUD, I imagine they can convert it to condominiums, you know with the...because they're the legal owners now.

CHIN: Uh huh.

KOON: And act...actually probably because...they probably could even uh, you know, stop Seattle Housing from managing it. And if they can just pull from under out under them...I think the legal ...the legal loophole is that you get uh they get these buildings for provide low income housing to serve people for tax credit. So that's what the incentive...you know, providing low income housing. But ah but they... but...but the way I figure it, I might wrong on this...they say they get the buildings for free over a mil a certain number of years, because they don't have to pay taxes. You know, they get tax cuts. So they actually acquire the buildings for free.

CHIN: Hmm!

KOON: Now you. Just take a step back. It means the political cronies of George W. Bush gets these buildings for free.

CHIN: How many tenants in the building?

KOON: It's approximately a hundred units, so most of the units have one or two people so maybe about a hundred to about a hundred and twenty people.

CHIN: And are they all low income people...or what are they?

KOON: They all low-income people. Now, they're kicking out the people who they [think] have more money. They think they have more money, so they kicking out. Well they actually didn't kick me out. They said I no longer qualify for rent subsidy. So I will have to pay the market rate, which is $1200. a month. Before that I was paying $154. a month.

C: The building you saved. Let's talk about that. That's located where?

K: 2016 1/2 7th Avenue South. Called the Republic Hotel. Built in the 1920's and the 1930's.

C: It had cockroaches and mice...?

K: When I first moved in it was an empty room with a cot and one small table. Um I said, you know I looked at the small table said the ... that would be a nice place to put the typewriter. Maybe I will take this room, since rent is only $60. a month, for a single occupant.

After I start cooking I had a lot of uninvited guests. They stay with me. Cockroaches and mice.

C: What did you have to cook on?

K: I have a hot plate. That didn't come with the room. I had to borrow from my mother…the hotplate. But they do have one of the washbasins in the corner of the room. It used to be like a single room hotel for travellers.

C: Bathoom down the hall?

K: Yes, bathroom down the hall. And a tubroom down the hall.

C: Was that clean?

K: Well, the relatively, for, you know, that kind of rent. However there was a 95 year old man, living you know there. He had to climb…there's no elevator. He had to climb the stairs every day. But you know, several people in their eighties, you know had to climb the stairs everyday.

C: Rents were so low, was it all Chinese…

KOON: They owned by several family associations, because they let the relatives rent there first. Okay?

C: Right.

K: It just so happens though, my mother's cousin is part owner of that building.

C: Um.

K: So they let me live there.

C: What happened to the bulditng to cause you to save it?

K: Well, the uh owners decided to uh uh renovate so that's because of incentive, because they can get a matching fund from the city. Which, I don't know what it is, I just make a rough guess, they you know, Needs over a hundred thousand dollars.

They found out I was a writer that wrote for the Seattle Chinese Post. So they said, well, you know, Koon, You know, you know you do an article for us. How were going to, you know, upgrade the living conditions of the dependents.

So I say "Yeah, that's a good idea." And they took me out to dinner, you know, the people, the housing people of Chinatown. Couple of young people. Those people that come to Chinatown to do good, you know. They mainly they come here to do good for themselves, you know.

So they says, "Koon, were going to make you the manager. When after we renovate it."

"That sounds good, you know."

The rooms are going to be bigger. You know, more modern, you know. All that. Then I thought about it a little while. "But what about those guys that can't come back that can't afford the rent. There'll be fewer people living because the rooms will be bigger. And what about future immigrants who, you know, come here to live? And I know that the reason people living here like my cousin's living here, that they want to save money on the rent, so they can buy a house. For the future, you know, so they can have kids, and grandkids in this country. So they want a house, you see.

So, I said, for these and other reasons, Maybe it's not a such a good idea to renovate.

I uh spoke up against it. The tv station KOMO caught the news of the story somehow, I don't know how, but they came to interview me on Prime Time Newstime three days in a row. They filmed my room. It just so happened they filmed my tv my little tv I got for ten dollars in my room. There's cockroach walking on the tv screen. They filmed that on Prime Time Newstime.

CHIN: What year is this?

KOON: This is 1992, I believe. Remember, I was not well at that time. And my psychiatrist, you know , he uh, he said, you know, "Koon," you know, "You're writing so well. I don't believe you have mental illness. At least not schizophrenia. I think you're pure bipolar. You really don't need anti-psychotic medication. We think your lithium will do." So he took me off my anti-psychotic medication. I slowly went off the deep end, you know, I became psycotic.

Then I went into the hospital. When I went into the hospital, they put an eviction notice on my room. So, I came home, I was evicted. The deputy the sheriff's deputy came to see me and says, "You know, I didn't really want to do this to you Mr. Woon. This is my job."

I said, "That's all right. In China, we do not kill the policeman, we kill the mayor."

(LAUGHTER)

C: And so you on tv for three days. What was the reporter from KOMO

KOON: Yeah. She was a Chinese woman.

CHIN: What was her name?

KOON: I can't remember now.

CHIN: And uhh

KOON: The funny incident was I considered myself a poet at that time. So I said, "I want to read a poem on tv. I think it's relavent." Well, one point of the poem is about the Republicans, were in power at that time, disappeared. One of the poem says, "Have the art/ Have the fart/Love and leave these lands.."

(LAUGHTER)

And then she says. "Oh we haven't got time for a whole poem. Maybe just read half a poem."

(laughter)

CHIN: Were these poems in a book of yours?

KOON: No not that poem. One's lost. When I was evicted I placed everything was lost. Except a doctor's stub, kept the uh At Luke's Pharmacy I gave to my…I get my medicine there I said, "Judy," you know, she works there. "Can you keep this box of stuff for me till I get…come ad pick it up?" She kept it there for me a long time. So I went back and got it.

CHIN: Hmmm! Ahh! Yeah.

KOON: But I lost a lot of writing that way.

CHIN: The book…I forget the name of the book that you…you gave me

KOON: THE TRUTH IN RENTED ROOMS? You mean my book?

CHIN: Yeah.

KOON: My poetry book. THE TRUTH IN RENTED ROOMS.

CHIN: Did you write about your rented room at the Republic Hotel?

KOON: There's a poem in there called A MOMENT IN MY RENTED ROOM. I compare myself to the astronaut. The room's so small it's like being in a space capsule.

≈•≈•≈•≈•≈•≈•≈•≈•≈•≈•≈•≈•≈•≈•≈•≈•≈•≈•≈•

A Moment in my rented room

I sometimes think of myself as an astronaut

In my compact, rented room and look upon the bookshelf

With its deep mathematics books for deeper space

As from a voyage one cannot return.

Then multiply by serval million men who cannot marry,

Men who cannot own home, or work, or go to college.

This is almost equal to the space effort.

But why all that money? I can go to Pluto bu just

Being in a bad mood.

Sometimes I think of the loneliness of deep space

In my rented room. The neighbors have busily gone off

To Epsilon Centauri or Galaxy X-2137 or to the 7-Eleven.

Sometimes I look at my 16-oz. Jar of coffee, I know

What the minimum daily requirements are. Cybernetics

Steers me to avoid collisions with black holes or stars,

And my hot plate sustains me with pinto beans and bacon rinds,

And on my mini-stereo, always the Blue Danube.

It is rainy today. My room is a bastion. I am filing

The sparse bars of prison. I am building a mental atom bomb.

I am designing spaceships. Multiply this by several million.

≈•

CHIN: What were the dimensions of your room?

KOON: About 10 x 12. I did all my cooking, eating, writing. I did my laundry. If the wet be out, I hang my laundry up, in the room, to dry.

I lived there for seven years. I was helping other people live there. I helped with things from the Government. My uncle family, my uncles younger brothers whole family came here, they lived there [at the Republic?] I taught my two cousins ESL and I taught a couple other women ESL for two years. No pay. Just volunteer. I did all the uh you know the financials… you know uhh legal errands for them. I took them to school. I took them to get jobs. I did everything like that. I helped them get adjusted to life in America.

CHIN: You said you worked in restaurants.

KOON: Yes. I began working in restaurants 12 years old. That's my family business. The whole thing is I learned how to do sidework, wash dishes, cook, wait on tables, manage restaurant. I essentially didn't quick work in restaurants. I was drunk 28 years old. (??) And even when I was a mental patient and in a health clinic, I volunteered to cook lunch. I cooked for 30 people in two hours time. All by myself. But we'd order the food, and cook the food, and served it, all in two hours. 30 people.

Yeah, in Seattle. Dotel. CDC Dotel. That's the worst characters in the mental health system.

CHIN: What's CDC?

KOON: Psychiatric Community Center or clinic Community Psychiatric Clinic or something like that.

CHIN: You said you worked in San Francisco also

KOON: Yes, in...in a restaurant. Soo it's....A Chinese-Filipino restaurant.

CHIN: Where was this restaurant locacated?

KOON: At Battery and California. Financial District.

CHIN: How long did you work there?

KOON: I worked there for about six months.

CHIN: So you were right here in Chinatown.

KOON: Yeah. Yeah. In Chinatown. I lived in the Grant Avenue. I stayed with my aunt. She had a flat on Grant Avenue. 1362 Grant Avenue...something like that. 1632 Grant Avenue. That was North Beach. Cuz you know that place very well.

CHIN: OH! YOU'RE A POET.

KOON: Right.

CHIN: YOU'RE RIGHT THERE IN NORTH BEACH.

KOON: That was before I did any literature. At all. I went there mainly to uh Ferlinghetti's bookstore after uh you know after work to read psychology books. Because I was slowly going crazy. I didn't know I was going crazy. But, I knew something was wrong. I was trying to read psychology books trying to figure myself out.

CHIN: Compare Chinatown Seattle with San Francisco. Was San Francisco more Chinese or less Chinese?

KOON: More Chinese. More Chinese. More real. You know, but, however, it's hard to make a living there. Because, you know, whenever you're more people competition labor competition keener. Wages are lower, you know, and the living space is smaller you know, and then here uhh it's not as much commerce but fewer people here. And then people can get jobs outside of Seattle's Chinatown.

CHIN: Did you enjoy San Francisco?

KOON: Yes, I did. The part of the time I was crazy. I was hospitalized. I was released out I lived in a half-way house in a Jackson and Fillmore, I believe.

CHIN: Oh, yeah.

KOON: You know where that is right? I lived there old Victorian house with 30 other uh you know, a colony there. Was called the Connor House. The cream of the crop of halfway houses. The uh…These are dropouts from Columbia, Berkeley, uh Yale

CHIN: Huh!

KOON: Mills College…I mean, I was with those ivy league schools…or kids. And I had the most money!

(Laughs)

CHIN: Hmm

KOON: Cuz I knew how to make money. I worked at a donut shop at night, nearby. In one of the poems of my book is a …it's called THE SPY'S RELIABLIBITY. It's based on my experience working at donut shop at night.

CHIN: Ah ha

KOON: You know why?

CHIN: Why?

KOON: Because there was uh there was actually Iranian chess master went there to play….chess. He was…he was whisper to me, he says, "They give me a drugs. 'nd they're…They're trying to control your mind.

(LAUGHTER)

≈•≈•≈•≈•≈•≈•≈•≈•≈•≈•≈•≈•≈•≈•≈•≈•≈•≈•≈•

The Spy's reliability…

He was at the corner donut shop; that was
his assignment. He watched the donut-
maker Buck and the chess players, in
particular the Iranian chess master; the other

hangers-on, the drug dealers and so forth were only of minor importance. He comes in the day, ostensibly to pay chess and talk of psychotherapies. At night he comes, ostensibly to read a book on economics by Samuelson. Everyone knows he is a spy, however, since most of them are spies themselves, and it takes one to know one, as the saying goes. The Fillmore District was full of spies, because the newspapers were a printed there, in all languages that were popular in the city.

He plays chess sometimes in off-hours at night, and on weekends when he pretends he can't sleep in his rooming house nearby, he comes to see Buck, to play chess and say his school books are driving him crazy. He purposely loses to Buck, a black guy who never really had time to study chess, and Buck will feel good and whisper things to him, that there's saccharine in the donuts in place of sugar, and that this little donut shop is really owned by a black church, not the little black guy they called Steve. The spy never seems to be prying. He always seems to be unimpressed, so that Buck tells more and more, juicier and juicier tidbits, hoping to make him happy...

The spy himself has had no communications with command for a long time. There could have been changes in command structure or channels of communication, breakdowns, paralysis due to infiltrations by hostile forces, or just an inadvertent oversight, meaning he is lost in the paperwork. Or, the most satisfactory explanation to him, he is so deep in the bowels of the investigations that he is miles under ground, beneath the beds of rivers and dinosaur fossils, so close to the fire itself that they don't dare jeopardize his cover...

The Iranian chess master plays the other players blindfolded, ten at a time, while smoking imported Iranian cigarettes. He of course has no chessboard; he just shouts his moves, the mind is all. The other players play him for money and they smoke Marlboros and Camels and Kents and drink coffee and eat saccharine donuts at the little tables in the Fillmore and Vallejo donut shop while cars go in four directions outside, occasionally a thug-thug teenaged music car slouches around the street corner slowly, like Yeat's Beast in his metaphysical poem to be reborn. The Iranian loses all ten games, and pays the money that has been wagered. It seems the money has petroleum stains on it. The Spy makes note of it.

Usually, unless one's a mole, a spy is to be transferred frequently so that his objectivity and consequent usefulness is not

jeopardized by inadvertent and undesirable attachments to his subjects. So, since the spy hasn't been notified of nay transfers, in fact, has had no communications whatsoever, he begins to think his cover has been blown, in a deep and profound way that could damage the entire apparatus, and more and more, he comes to the unattractive but forced conclusion that he's been written off, forgotten and abandoned, and therefore he is free at last, to see what he sees without a fixed format of interpretation, to simply live among the people as if they were his brothers and sisters. It is difficult to say which is the cause and which the effect, the net result in that when Buck asks him to play chess, he says yes. He's no longer reliable...

≈•

CHIN: Did the fact there were more people more Chinese around did you find that stimulating or depressing?

KOON: Well I think in uh in San Francisco, you know, there's uh...uh...uh. Things are more open. Everything's open. Life styles. Uh, you know. Different persuasions. Different philosophies. All things are more open. Different cultures. More open than...Seattle. Little bit more. Seattle's you know quite liberal in the old days. Now it's got too much political correct.

(CHIN LAUGHS)

CHIN: In the old day's it was more liberal. When were the old days?

KOON: Well, you know, you were here, back in the late 60's early 70's. That's when you wrote for the SEATTLE Magazine. I remember you then… The first time I saw you, you were at the Sky [River] Folk Rock Festival playing the flamingo guitar with a bunch of gypsies. And the second time I saw you was at the Last Exit on Brooklyn. And somebody says well that's Frank Chin, he's a…he's a writer of the SEATTLE magazine.

CHIN: Hmm

KOON: He was my next door neighbor from Aberdeen, Washington. He was in English. He was an English major. I was a math major, so I didn't, I was not into literature at that time, so. I was not into literature at al until I was 30. That's because, after mental illness I had such, you know, difficult feelings.

CHIN: UM HMM.

KOON: I would try to write in my diary, you know, "I feel so terrible. I wonder why" 'nd this and that. "If I had…If I could do this, I would do this." "I hope things will be better tomorrow." Jus' Jst write down my feelings. And over a five year period, I started writing little images. "If that is a toilet, I'm flushed." That's how my poetry started. Really bad, like that, you know? As bad as toilet unflushed. That's how my poetry grew.

CHIN: Right.

KOON: Then in 1985 decide to take a poetry workshop from uh Nelson Bentley at University of Washington. The first month I was there, some kids in the room started a magazine. So they said, Well, Can we have one of your poems? You know it was with in the first year they published. And then they uh Then I decide to enter the Bumbershoot. I was chosen at Bumbershoot. I was the kind of people as one of the three chosen. So. Bentley says, "Well, you know, maybe you should uh, you know, try your hand at poetry. And then uh. That was 1985. I didn't collect enough poems until 1998, to have my first book published. And so far it's the only book I got published.

CHIN; Uh huh.

KOON: Uh huh.

CHIN: With what publisher?

KOON: Kaya in New York city. Which is mainly a publisher of Asian diaspora.

CHIN: What was the first thing of mine you read? (Laughs) If you have read anything of mine at all.

KOON: Yeah, I think I read uh . I don't remember if I read the whole thing was The CHICKECOOP CHINAMAN

CHIN: Yeah. Yeah. Yeah. How did that strike you?

KOON: Well you know uh. I really don't remember. Mental illness did a lot of things to my memory. The years of my life I don't remember. Back in 1996, I was convinced I killed two people in my sleep. But don't remember who. For two years I was absolutely convinced I killed two people.

CHIN: Wow!

KOON: I walked around every day. I wonder, you know, if they're going to get me. Get me for it, you know. So I must've killed 'em in my sleep.

CHIN: Wow!

KOON: I threw them off my roof. I know I did. You know, so.

CHIN: My writing drove you crazy!

(HUGE LAUGHTER)

I thank you for remembering me. The Last Exit. Wow.

KOON: See the things that are a long time ago remember better than things recently. That's that's. I think I got electric shock treatments. That's what that's something, you get a short term memory.

CHIN: You, yourself play guitar…

KOON: Yes. I play the blues. Folk and blues and rock'n'roll, yeah. I gave you a cd you can play it yeah.

CHIN: I sent it home already.

KOON: (Sings) Unchain my heart/ Baby let me be/ Darling you don't care about me/ Unchain my heart/ Baby, set me free...

CHIN: Now, we'll see if we got anything.

CHIN; Anything I missed?

KOON: We can make aother session sometime. You can go over your notes and then see what else you need and talk about some more. Yeah.

CHIN: Oh, ah! You said the Locke family is settled mainly in Seattle...

KOON: Oh, ahh... in the state of Washington. It started in Hoquiam my great grandfather's the godfather of the Locke family. He came to Hoquiam, Washington. The mayor of Hoquiam , Washington when was to his village is because, five hundred men to come over here. One of them was Gary Locke's grandfather.

CHIN: One was Gary Locke's grandfather.

KOON: That's right. My great grandfather brought him over here.

CHIN: Okay Gary Locke's grandfather

KOON: Yeh.

CHIN: is different from your grandfather.

KOON: Right. But they're the same clan. The Locke clan.

CHIN; And there are other Locke's in the area?

KOON: Yeah, there many Lockes that settled in the small towns. Aberdeen. Hoquiam. Satsup, Raymond, Centralia, you know, Elmira and uh up in Seattle. Then it branched out to California. In fact the main manager at San Francisco Chinatown, was a Locke, was a relative of mine. He was responsible for the Miss Chinatown Pageant in San Francisco.

CHIN: And so. Does the Locke family in Washington duplicate the Locke family in the vailage?

KOON: They're all descendants from the people in the three villages. The Locke family in the villages, in China.

CHIN: So there Locke famiy in three villages. What are the names of the three villages?

KOON: I can't remember. Two I don't remember. The third…Nom On, is my village. See Non is the next village. I don't remember the third one.

CHIN: It's all around Toishan?

KOON: Yes, in Toishan county. Just like we have King County here. Most of the Chinese immigrants in this country are originally from Toishan because. They had kind of a war there. And they had a famine very badly one year, so they all came America.

CHIN: My geography sort of messed up so, I know in Kwangtung Province there's Chungshan…

KOON: Chungshan is next to us.

CHIN: AHH!

KOON: Next to Toishan. Un hmm.

CHIN: And theres Lihoi?

KOON: Lihoi…?

CHIN: Jihoy?

KOON: Since I left China at 11, I don't know much geography.

CHIN: Your life in the village was really all in the village or how far out of the village did you travel? Say you were going on a holiday…

KOON: Well we generally. I go my maternal. My mother's side of the family. That's just three miles away. I would walk there and see my uncles. Usually people, in the old days, people usually very seldom more than a hundred miles from their own place. Because the transportation and communications so poor.

I did not leave my village at all until we went to..immigrated to Canton. Which is like a hundred miles away.

CHIN: When you walked 3 miles to wherever you walk, did you walk alone?

KOON: Yeah. It was safe. I mean it was safe at that time yeah. It was under Communism. There's only one scary part, there was a…house you know that didn't seem much windows that it was very dark inside. And people whisper to you, to kids, says uh, you know, "Be careful you walk by there. Fot mahngs live there!" What the hell's a fot mahng? I never until about now, you know it's a crazy person. They lock'em up. They don't have mental hospitals. They just lock'em up in a house somewhere and they feed'em, you know. And come to think of it I'm a fot mahng myself.

(LAUGHTER)

CHIN: Luckily you have a house with windows. Could you see mountains from where you were?

KOON: Uhh let's see. No. Hills. Just hills. Toishan means "a raised mound" Elevated mound.

CHIN: Oh, "Sahn" mountain.

KOON: Yeah. Hills. Toishan.

CHIN: You could see the Pearl River?

KOON: Not from where I was. We have to go to Canton. We lived in Canton for two years, actually swim in the mouth of the Pearl River. We saw dragonboat races...in the uh in the uh Pearl River.

CHIN: Do you remember Chinese New Years?

KOON: Yeah, Yeah. That's the big thing in the kid's life. You get 'lucky money,' I mean that's about the only time you get big money, that's the only time you play poker for real.

(Laughter)

CHIN: Did they have celebrations did you do lion dances or dragon...

KOON: Well not in the villages too much. I think the women did the flower drum songs there were the girls who were dressed up and put on their drums and dance and play the drums. I think the men did the acrobatics the tai-chi the kung fu whatever. Rumor has it my dad always carried the first flag in the village, during the holidays. He was uh this is what my maternal grandmother says, you know how the Chinese talk, they talk indirectly.

CHIN: Right.

KOON: The doorway has a little… jamb atop you know.

CHIN: Yeah.

KOON: You're tall for a Chinese, right? You're fairly tall right? My dad's not that tall, he's only five eight. So he's not as tall as the door…the top the door right?

But my grandmother would say to me, she says, "You're father's so tall, that when he goes through the door, he has to nod [lower] his head." What she's saying to me is, "He is the leader. When people see him they have to nod their head." Chinese…everything like that. Coding. They do not let you know for sure what they mean. So all your life you cannot know for sure what's happening. If you know that'd be a danger to yourself.

CHIN: Did you bai sun to the family?

KOON: Oh, yeah, yeah, yeah. Right! Right!

CHIN: Describe that. Did you set out tea for the dead?

KOON: Oh yeah, we uh. Generally you boil a chicken with the head on it. And then ah (coffeehouse is filling up.) And then you bring uh, you know, food and you make offering…incense and you put your hands together and you supplicate several times. And then you uh…after you uh…after your prayers and then you can share the food. And you get to eat the food there.

CHIN: ALL YOU HAVE TO DO IS PRPARE A CHICKEN AND RICE?

KOON: Mostly chicken, yeah. Anything that you like to eat that's good. Is it a good food. Suppoesdly your ancestors and supposedly in Heaven they cannot eat but they can…they live off the fragrance. The incense fragrance is a food. So that's how they could eat.

And you could anything that you eat they want to use in heaven, you make paper offerings and burn them, right?

CHIN: Right.

KOON: You burn money. Hell Bank Notes and things like that.

CHIN: Yes. Okay. Ah! There's a map over there. Yeah. Yeah.

KOON: You know what ThinkingChicken means, Frank, you know your … your ….

CHIN: My e-mail address?

KOON: Do you know what that comes from?

CHIN: ThinkinChicken?

KOON: Yeah.

CHIN: No.

KOON: You don't know where that comes from? What do you call that when you know something by ...by sixth sense. What do you do you know that. ESP? What do you call that?

CHIN: Awww!

KOON: When you know something by ESP? You know what I mean. Like a mindreader, you know, right?

In China, our teacher said, "Look at China. That's the shape of a rooster." See that's the head of a rooster. That's a chicken, man! Do you know what chicken means? In China?

CHIN: No.

KOON: Nay Hew hong goy muh? Goy!

CHIN: Goy?

KOON: Goy means strategy!

CHIN: Awww!

KOON: Thinking chicken, man! Chinese strategy!

CHIN: (LAUGHS) WOW! I did'nt know that...I thought that...yeah. So, I just hit on a name. And it turned out to be a good name.

KOON: That's the way language works.

CHIN: Yes.

KOON: If you're a Polick you pick that up

CHIN: Cuz you know, come with me, (walks across room to globe) look at the map. Now I see this as a camel's head.

KOON: Uh huh.

CHIN: And the Yellow the Wong Haw is…forms the camel's back.

KOON: Um hmm.

CHIN: And Leongshan Marsh is right there.

KOON: Um hmm. Um hmm.

CHIN: But look at where the camel's looking. Right at Korea.

KOON: Uh huh. Well, before this is the rooster. The head here.

CHIN: Yeah.

KOON: Now, when you got a Mongol sitting on your chicken what do you do? (pause) That's time to worry, buddy!

(LAUGHTER)

CHIN: It seems there dual meanings for everything you can say or or or…

KOON: But that's Taoism. That's the Tao. That's the Tao.

You know the particle at the end of a sentence. They said they all say "um-muh" "how um how ah."

CHIN: Oh oh! You said uh. There was. "Sick jaw fon may uhh."

KOON: Um hm.

CHIN: And the answer is…

KOON: Gee gun uhh.

CHIN: Jur (the city dialect) gun uhh.

Oh, what's that mean?

KOON: Gee is control. Aw means the chairman. The chairman of the control. Means uh it's under control. I'm handling it okay. It means. "Have you eaten yet?" "Did you overcome?"

CHIN: Aha.

KOON: When people when they finish. They go (claps hands) Heck guh luh! That means "Done!"

CHIN: I thought it was. "Let's eat!"

KOON: When they finish doing something they say (clap hands) "Heck luh." If you ask them if you build a house, "Heck luh. Jang goong luh."

CHIN: I'm ashamed to say I guess I don't know Chinese at all.

There're these other shadow meanings or other meanings

KOON: I urge you to read, just if you have time, one of these days, read Wittgenstein what he means by private language.

All language. It's a hopeless task for philosophers who have a hundred years to invent a perfect language with every grammatically correct sentence has a definite meaning.

But it was a futile effort because every language would generate its own metaphors in time. That's the darkhorse of language out there.

If it's in use long enough it will generate metaphors. In the country evolving language constantly.

CHIN: Right.

KOON: If you read the Tao te Ching. There's a lot of hidden language in the Tao De Ching. "Ruling a large nation is like cooking a small fish."

What does cooking a small fish in Chinese Cantonese. "Gee siyew yur.." Siyew yur (small fish) means "small talk" means "conspiracy" controlled conspiracy. "Ruling the big country is to control the conspiracies."

Chinese languages. There are 50 thousand characters in the dictionary, approximately. To be a literate person you need about five thousand of them. So a lot of words, you know, these bigger words I only went to five years of British school. And I only speak to my parents and they speak to me like a little kid. So a lot of adult words I don't understand.

However there are things I understand that even a scholar don't understand.

Depends on what kind of background ....of family background comes up.

CHIN: Ah, let's see… "mo bahn fot."

KOON: Means uh, "without…" "unable to do something" without the ability to ..without the means to do something."

CHIN: Does it have another meaning?

KOON: Uh…Mo bon fot. Means….uh No method to do something. Uh…generally that's pretty neutral. When you say that. There's another way of saying that. "Oy mo nung jaw" Which means I love to do it but I can't help it." I mean, "I'm not able to… I sure wish I could help you but I can't." "Oy mo mung jaw."

That's a more polite way of saying.

CHIN: When did your grandmother die?

KOON: She died when I was….I think she died in about 1975 at 83 age 83…I was like 27.

I'll tell you something, very strange. That night I had a dream. I saw an old woman laying down on a dead floor to sleep. I said isn't that kind of strange, the floor is cold, you know. Sleeping on a dirt floor is kind of cold. So I put a blanket over her.

And two weeks later, my parents told me that my grandmother had died…that night! That very night!

CHIN: Were you closer to your grandmother or to your parents?

KOON: My grandmother, yeah. My poem THE MEMORY OF THE HANDS is in the SEATTLE REVIEW. Nelson Bentley put that in there. He says. "We're very lucky to get this poem." So… "Very lucky to get this poem."

It's about me and my grandmother leaving China.

≈•

The Memory **of hands**

In memory of my grandmother

I. In Water Buffalo Time

Honey-Auntie collects bees in her palm:

When she says Go! They fly off to sue the flowers,

And when she says Come back! They roll their honey-

Bellies in her hand.

Uncles arc in race paddies, itching where leeches suck

Their legs.

I sprinkle Grandmothers's garden of bokchoy, cabbages,

And wintermelons heavy like little buddhas.

Grandmother gets wood and gossip from Firewood-auntie,

And pays her a few bronze coins to light incense.

Both women's husbands died three decades ago.

Leaving them the void of Confucian hands.

At dusk my grandmother trots out in her bound feet to retrieve

The drying vegetables hung on a bamboo pole like the character

Jen (people).

The sun drops behind the last rice paddy

As the water buffalo sinks in the vegetable pond,

Dropping dung for black shrimps.

And at last grandmother draws the mosquito net

In the lychee-pit night.

II. Sampan

A journey in yellow water. I am sick

And grandmother tells me to think of not moving.

Think of a place far away like Gimshan, she says.

Do not move against the river and you will be still.

Your head was so big we used forceps,

And now you are a cavern

For three bowls of rice and pig's feet stewed in rice vinegar!

Grandmoter is not moving although the boat moves.

She tells me to think of lemon.

The boatman, pushing the river bottom with his long bamboo pole,

Carries all the land he cares for in his sampan.

As I become better, I awe at his calves.

The river I know must have fish.

The fish must look up at the shadow that moves.

The fish move in a moving river,

But I am stil because grandmother is still.

We are leaving the village for Canton.

The chrysanthemums are in bloom just now.

And Gimshan is where I must soon go.

III. The World's Longest Alley

For a snip of cloth Grandmother took my hand

And led through bicycle-laden streets,

Past shoppers by fours, past wine and vinegar stores.

Buses overtook us.

And finally, walking as far as three rolls

Of cloth would unroll,

We arrived at the entrace of the world's longest alley,

Where vendors on both sides set up

Painted fans, brilliantly glazed pottery,

And cloth of every color
As they haggled with shoppers,

Squeezing the alley like a tourniquet on a blood vessel.

Grandmother: "The five colors blind the eye!"

But she doesn't heed Lao Tsu and slides her fingers

On the rolls of exquisite cloth.

We hear it is exported.

But there are no candy vendors, though there's a man

Who has taught his monkey to beg with a tipped hat.

The alley is long as a conversation with a river.

In the colorful blur, she assents to an ice-cream bar.

I am then happy for coming along,

For the first time I see

Grandmother as a maiden of sixteen,

Her young eyes dazzled by the dowry of cloth.

IV. The Momory of Hands

If you fold a piece of paper once, then unfold it,

It will tend toward the folded position. That's because

The paper has "memory."

The memory of hands, of ancient vine,

My monsoon eyes, my face, tilled by fingers.

A chicken plucked gently naked.

Hands , unable to sign a legal signature,

Close the fan,

And draw the mosquito net.

At the Hong Kong International Airport, I took a mental

Photograph fo my grandmoter. A young gir swrings free of

Her mother's hand and runs along, laughing.

Her index finger wrote a whorl on my back to designate an ox.

My hands, curved upward to suggest valley of space,

Would squeeze water,

Would cling to ancient vine,

Would throw

A marble across the river.

The loudspeaker aannounces, announces last call, last call,

Third-aunt says hurry, hurry, or you will miss your future.

The past folds up like an origami bird,

Will not dissolve like candy.

Grapes cling to the vine, hands weave bamboo baskets,

Hands supplicate and light incense,

Buddha holds her in his palm.

I fold paper for hands of ancient vine,

Hands that couldn't come along.

And hands will open gates if I should return.

≈•

CHIN: How old were you when you were reunited with your parents?

KOON: I was twelve. Eleven something. Yeah. 1960.

CHIN: And did you have good relations with your parents?

KOON: Over the years I became, you know, more distant from them because of the uh, you know, Chinese family, are patriarchal, they own it, they want you to…You know, the first generation immigrants, they want you to go to the restaurant business or real estate. Okay? I was like you, I wanted to be a, I don't know, I wanted to be mathematician. They didn't see anything in that. They said to me, my dad always say, "How much does a professor make? I make 30 thousand a year!" You know. At that time PhD's were making 17 thousand a year. He says. "I make 30 thousand a year! I mean, How much does a professor make?" and he's always saying, when I read books, novels and stuff like that for school, he says, you know. "You're always doing things that don't need to be done."

CHIN: Umm.

KOON: You know, I was trying to play the guitar, I was trying to read books, trying to learn how to play chess. He says, "You're always trying to do things that don't need to be done."

CHIN: How do you say that in Chinese?

KOON: "Seng yee do um hung soy guh!"

CHIN: Ah!

KOON: Seng yee dole um hung soy guh

CHIN: Um hung soy guh.

KOON: Um hung soy guh.

CHIN: Huh! Aha! Did your mother participate in judging you?

KOON: Yah! Yeah. She's at that…she uh she said that…she just wanted me to make so much money, so I just got mad, I says, "Okay, by the time I'm thirty I'm going to have a million dollars. Will you be happy then?"

Course, I'm never going to have a million dollars.

CHIN: (laughs) Yeah. Join the club.

KOON: But uh one of my brothers did have a million and when he got a divorce, his wife got half of it. So, you know what he did? He remarried her!

(Laughs)

CHIN: So your brothers and sisters were born in America?

KOON: Um hmm.

CHIN: Are you close to any of them?

KOON: No, not really. Not really. Over the years because the financial transactions in the family. Well…I don't want to get too much into that part of it because I don't have all the facts.

CHIN: So let's stick with your uhhh. You say you're publishing magazines and and uh…

KOON: I did. I did. The uh now I'm not uh. I'm completely in debt. Heavily into debt. And then I…I thought it was easy, you know, if you get a good author, you know, it'll sell like hotcakes. I mean, you know, maybe a big publisher, you know, will buy your copyright. Sell like hotcakes.

So that sort of thing. I knew nothing about it. I get hypomania. I still get hypomania, when my judgement's kind of impaired. I spend too much money. I do things…**the thing about me is I was born a village boy, when I give my word, I follow my word.** To the tee. I promise somebody that I'd do something even though it was made out of bad judgement I still try to fulfill my obligation. So. That's the way I am. So.

CHIN: What's the difference between you …yeah…what's the difference between you and me? We both say we're Chinese.

We're both Chinese-American.

KOON: The thing is, Frank, the uh. I don't know who wrote that poem, but uh, something to the effect that something about, you'll walk into a room one day. You'll see your friends there. And they all have their seats. Everyone's got their own place in the universe. So the you're Chinese, I'm Chinese, you're a liitle bit different than me, in the Chinese way. I'm a little bit different than you, in Chinese way. That doesn't mean you're a worse Chinese you're not as qualified Chinese as I am. Or I'm a better Chinese than you are. You're obviously more noted About the Chinese in this country, than I am. And you know, and so. In that way you're better Chinese because you're uh I mean, you more, I mean,have spread the word about China…your version of it, I mean, which is good, I mean it's like, I mean, they would, okay, et me. Let me put it in terms of uh an anecdote, Okay?

We have a Chinese-American restaurant. What in the old days we called a chop suey house, okay? The people that used to eat in a chop suey house, they'd come to eat chop suey and chow mien, right?

If you give 'em some real Chinese food, and "What is this garbage! I don't wanta have to…I don't order." And "This is not Chinese food!" I mean, "That's something you eat. But it's not what I eat. It's not what I consider Chinese food." You see? See what I mean? If I give'em the real stuff they would think, they would not take it, see. You give'em the stuff….you lead them in. See? You lead them to me. I give'em the real stuff.

(Laughter)

CHIN: Yeah.

KOON: Yeah I mean. That's the way it goes. You don't wanta. I mean when you want to send a Chinese ambassador overseas, he has to speak English. He's got to present the good side of China to people. He doesn't say, well you know, China's just as bad as you guys. You are criminals, you have racism, you have this and that. We got arsonists, and we have disaster on our mind! We sell fake blood in hospitals. You know. You want to come China to do business?

(Laughter)

They say "Oh, we can give you tax credit. We can give you credit breaks. We can subsidize your company. We'll give you loans. You know. You come to help us develop our country.

You coming to help us, man. We want you in China. See? But...but that's the way it is in the world.

CHIN: Have you been mistaken for Gary Locke?

KOON: Not mistaken, but they uh they uh maybe a couple of times, people uh when I mentioned I'm related to him they will say, "You look alike."

CHIN: Do you have any contact with him?

KOON: Not since he threatened to put me in jail.

(Laughter)

CHIN: Oh!

KOON: He called the cops on me. They came up to my room to try to arrest me.

CHIN: This was when...When?

KOON: No, in 1992. I was going off the deep end, because my doctor told me I'm mensan (?)

CHIN: Which room?

KOON: Well at the uh at the uh Republic Hotel. The tenement building. He was King County Executive at that time.

And he said. You know, I call him up on the phone every morning. I says uh. He says uh. He said, "Rumor has it your America's best mathematician." I said, "Yeah, provided you're the President of the United States."

(Laughter)

CHIN: You know when I first met him. He was a student at Franklin High School. And we got to talking he doesn't remember it but he said that he wanted to be President of the United States. And after seeing him, his career his rise through politics and his developing charm...and he really is, he's developed this quality. I...I think he could be President of the United States.

KOON: Yeah. Yeah. He could be. The only thing is the uh, you know how it is, the uh is not ready for a minority, is not ready for a woman. At this point.

CHIN: I think what's holding him back, is there are no newspapers in town, here. I mean no Chinese newspapers ...the Chinese newspapers the Japanese newspapers really aren't real.

But you say you used to write for the Chinese Post?

KOON: In the English version. They become now days in a weekly, you know.

I was the first reporter for them. Assunta Ng. Assunta Ng. But she just wanted me to write tourist articles. I wrote a story on jade, Chinese museums, Chinese furniture things like that.

I did have a uh Asian American writers, the Seattle area, the special issue. I don't think you were in town, at that time.

CHIN: How much did she pay you?

KOON: Thirty dollars an article. That was a lot of money back then. 1990…I mean for me I was only getting SSI was three hundred dollars a month. So that's one tenth my income for a week's work. You know. cuz it took me a long time to write. I've always been a slow writer.

I'd research my stuff well. And I'd, you know, she said, "You know, you're a good writer, but you're too slow. I'd better let you go."

You know she has got to have the article every month every week, you know.

CHIN: So you know Assunta.

KOON: She said… she was a little bit afraid of me, because at the uh when I went off the deep end, I uh, I wanted them to put an ad in the paper. "My father's name is not Fay Lung Woon but George Bush is the President of the United States." And they didn't to put that ad in there.

And then I said uh, "Why not?"

They said uh, "Well we just don't want to put that ad in there."

"Isn't that against freedom of speech?"

"You get your lawyer and talk to us."

I says, "Okay. When you want a lawyer, you get a lawyer. When I want a lawyer, I get a gun!"

(Laughs)

C HIN: Okay! We got a lot of stuff.

KOON: Yeah. So anyway, I gotta call somebody.

CHIN: Do you consider yourself a Buddhist?

KOON: Well, you know, Frank is uh, you know the philosophies, you know in the world, that uh could work for a lot of people , you know, in the uh I'm kind of uh eclectic you know, I mean, the uh. Essentially I believe that if it's alternative life, it'd be sort of like string theory, you know. Alternative, parallel universes. But I don't know, you know, it's just mathematically convenient, I mean. It's beautiful. To have that kind of conception, that you know. If you really really attract me, I just say, it's impossible to know.

Okay, let me put it this way.

There's a joke that goes like this: Life has always been in doubt. Only fools assure the case...." You know. Have you seen that? "Yes, absolutely."

"Life has always been in doubt. Only fools assure the case. "

CHIN: Right.

KOON: Have you heard that? Yes, absolutely. //he visited a mental asylum, asked the director, How can you tell when you bring somebody in here that he's really really crazy?

He says he's about appear by the window. There's a thimble, there's a dog, there's a bucket.

"Oh I get it." So the same guy so when I used a symbol to build a backup I used a bucket. No no no, the same guy unplugged the tub because he wanted the seat next to the window.

We walk up past the sign to the empty Tokuda Pharmacy and the other empty Panama Hotel storefronts up the hill, turn to walk down the broad brick side of the Panama on what used to be a red brick alley as lick as spit in the rain, but today the air is humid but not wet. Instead of a wall on the other side of the Panama, was a parking lot. Koon's voice bounces lightly off elements in the Panama's red brick that vibrate to his words about the Chinese tenants of the International Terrace across the street from Panama's front, composing a petition to restore garbage down-chutes on every floor that were a service that tempted the elderly tenants the tenants getting rickety and rickety to take apartments and fill the building. Tenants of the fifth, fourth and third floor should not be forced to walk down to second floor to chute their garbage into the dumpster, and elevator back up to their floor. The petition was all written in Chinese and they didn't want it thrown out because the manager's don't know how to read. So Koon translated the tenants' petition. And that was when the managers started to pry him out of the building. We come to Jackson Street. Maynard to the left. 6th Ave to the right. I want noodles at Mike's Noodles on Maynard. I can see the old half a block wide and a block long Uwajimaya, now a gallery of Asian antiques. I want to show Koon the bronze crazy eyed Kwan Kung showing his teeth and holding a pot of gold ingots in his left hand, disguised as the Buddha of Seven Stars, symbolized by a pagoda in his fighting right hand, but the pagoda is Monkey in disguise.

Have I gone too far in interpreting Kwan Kung? I want to see Koon's face when I show him the bronze. I interrupt his story and take him across the street. The Kwan Kung is gone. He's been moved to the more expensive store in Bellevue.

and left on Jackson against traffic to Maynard turn right and cross on Maynard to Mike's Noodle House.

≈•

KOON: I can sympathize. For ten years, Frank, I uh I couldn't play the guitar, either. Cuz the medicine. It gave me no ability to feel. I laid on paper Zombie I just eat. No appetite, I go to sleep, it's like passing out on the street or something. And I'd sleep for 36 hours at a time. And I had anxiety so bad I couldn't sit still. I couldn't stand. I couldn't wait. I couldn't read. You know, I couldn't listen to music, you know, I couldn't do anything. Wherever I am, I want to be somewhere else. Whenever I get there, I want to be somewhere else. If I was doing one thing, I want to do something else.

The only thing that saved me was I forced myself to sleep24 hours 36 hours as long as I sleep just to avoid that anxiety. They tried everything. All the drugs that they uh, acupuncture , you know, everything, everything. Nothing worked. Therapy… nothing worked.

So as I had no feelings, of course, no sexual feelings, no uh, you know, no uh, . Just total nothing! Just uh total zombie like. And that was not just people like me, you lived you lived the Thorizine shuffle people like this (he hangs his arms and lifts and plants his feet) ghosts all day long. I wasn't so bad. I was on Lithium I just shake all the time. And people thought I was afraid! Nervous or scared! I mean, you do feel you're scared because you're shaking. But, am I scared, you know, cuz I'm shaking like a leaf.

CHIN: WHEN DID YOUR MEMORY BEGIN?

KOON: About four. Right before I went to school. Because I only remember three times in the village pond from they pull me out of the village pond, and my grandmother comes and said uh and she buys, you know, burns incense and pray to the gods and that they, you know, protect me from falling into the pond again, you know.

Then she finally took me to this school. I was four and she begged the teacher. "My grandson's not yet five but accept him as a student cuz I can't watch'em. I have to go to work in the rice paddies, and this and that. And he might drown in the village pond." So then the teacher accepted me. I started school early. A year. And then I was such a hyperactive kid I never, I remember never be in my seat. And then finally they have me repeat…I passed kindergarten, then I had to repeat the first grade cuz I couldn't, you know, sit still.

CHIN: HOW MANY STUDENTS WERE IN THE FIRST GRADE WITH YOU? This was right in the village?

KOON: Yeah, yeah. In the village school. Yeah. We had to walk uh. Well here's the routine in the village. You get up in the morning and you actually cook a full meal for breakfast, rice and everything. You eat that, and you get one canteen of water. That's all you get. One canteen of water. Plastic canteen of water. Of course it's boiled water. There's a lot of germs in it, you know. Dysentery. All kinds of diseases. That costs money to boil your water. Cuz where you gonna get the wood. You have to pay for the wood. So it cost you money. So that all you're allowed, just one canteen of water to go school. And that's all the school allows you to bring. And you have to ratio that for the whole day in school. So you don't want to drink it too fast. What people do is put dessicated plums in there. You had a dessicated plum?

CHIN: LOM?

KOON: Mooey. Him shurn mooey. Sweet'n'sour mooey. So you start stretch the water, cuz there's a thirst quencher, see?

CHIN: Him shuren mooey?

KOON: That's Toishan. Tim shurn mooey, that's Cantonese.

CHIN: I GUESS I SPEAK MORE CANTONESE THAN TOISHANESE.

KOON: There's Sam yup Say yup. I don't know which is which. But it's pretty close. When I went in the village in Canton took me about two months I get used to the Cantonese right away.

But here when we speak Toishanese, all the Cantonese people, they "Non ting? Ho non ting. Gaw dee Toishan law. Ho non ting." It's "difficult to listen to."

CHIN: OH, "NON TENG." Yeah. Okay.

KOON: well let me tell you this, Frank. Being Chinese is not what you look like. Even you could be a white person. It's in the heart, man. It's in the heart. It's in the heart, you know why. You, you're really Chinese. I mean, if I'm Chinese, you're Chinese. Now, I say that from my heart.

Some of my white friends have more Chinese than my brothers. The way they treated me. I…I wouldn't call them Chinese.

It's like that poem I was trying to write, you know, my grandmother spent 32 years trying to distinguish between us all, you know. It's like that, I mean, you know uh. If you're Chinese you can zone into another Chinese. My uncle, he immigrated when he was twelve years old to Peru. He came back…We sponsored him he came to this country when he was 50. And he said wherever he went, I mean that he spoke Spanish, man! Pure Spanish! He spoke Chinese perfectly! And Spanish. Not a word of English. So he goes to Yakima he was supposed to work. He just goes there. Guess where he went. When he got lost, he went to the police station.

Says "I'm looking for so and so. My other relatives in Ellensburg, at a restaurant there. I'm looking for so and so, so they brought him to the restaurant.

CHIN: Okay were in school. How large is the school?

KOON: Well there's six grades. There's a grade school. I was in…first second grade. Up till the third grade, in the village maybe spend about the first semester in the third grade, then a maybe about twenty thirty each room, and then that. But sometimes we have the big room. Like everybody's in the same room, I think math. Something like that. I remember. Cuz we had a math bee, which is like a spelling bee. You go up there, choose sides, you go up there do problems. I remember I was always the first one chosen.

Because I last…outlast everybody. I solve all the problems. I never get to sit down.

CHIN: WAS IT A TWO STORY BUIDLING OR A SINGLE STORY BUILDING?

KOON: Single story.

CHIN: Tile roof?

KOON: Yeah. Yeah. Tile roof. It's a kind of a maybe built after the Communist took over. The first thing we did was calisthenics. The whole school did calisthenics out in the schoolyard, you know?

CHIN: Concrete blocks?

KOON: Either brick on the ground or uh dirt ground. I remember uh the back the school there's a bunch of trees, you know. I don't know the big trees got little berries on them. We called'em yoong see in China. The teachers would like…cuz it's semi-tropical it's very hot. So we sometimes have a…uh…like a uh literature class. We have it out underneath a tree. All these kids, you know, the teacher would tell a story. That was….that was the fun part. Nice and cool. You don't have to sit, and you sort of shift around with your friends.

CHIN: THE BERRY TREES THAT YOU SAT UNDER. WERE THEY TALL TREES OR

KOON: They were massive. They're not too tall but they were. Just massive.

CHIN: SPREAD OUT. DID THE BERRIES FALL ON YOU.

KOON: There were a lot of 'em on the ground. I don't know if they fall on you when you're just there. But there are a lot of'em on the ground. Yeah.

CHIN: DID YOU EAT THE BERRIES?

KOON: No. They were not edible.

CHIN: WHAT COLOR WERE THEY?

KOON: They're red.

CHIN: AND THE TEACHERS DO YOU REMEMBER ANY TOF THE STORIES THEY TOLD YOU?

KOON: Well, you know they told us about the uh when the Japanese occupied China, they uh, you know, the uh the people had nothing to eat. So cook up their little babies and ate sold...make candy of them and sold it to some...I don't know if it's true or not, but then you know.

CHIN: YEAH.

KOON: I don't know if it's true or not, but then you know. They tell all kinds of weird stories. See, they just dramatize how bad the Japanese were, see? You know. Might not be true. They exaggerate. You know what I mean. Nobody liked the Japanese at that time.

(LAUGHTER)

KOON: That's another. That's a tactic...political tactic to shift the blame to somebody else. Maybe somebody was didn't like Communism so shifted the blame on...

CHIN: ON THE JAPANESE

KOON: to Japanese. Scapegoating.

CHIN: AND THERE WEREN'T ANY JAPANESE AROUND?

KOON: No. No. Absolutely not. Zero.

CHIN: HOW LONG WAS THE DAY AT SCHOOL?

KOON: Let's see, we uh we go there early in the morning. I don't...Seven or eight. And then we come home to lunch for an hour. Then we have to go back. And then uh. Then uh. And then have to. It's about as long as long as the grade school year. Except on Saturdays, we have to go half a day. That's the routine in China and in Hong Kong. You have to go to school half a day on Saturday.

CHIN: DID YOU WEAR UNIFORMS?

KOON: Not in the village in Hong Kong I did. I went to private school in Hong Kong.

CHIN: SAY YOU GOT OUT OF SCHOOL AROUND THREE O'CLOCK.

KOON: Right. Right.

CHIN: AND YOU GO HOME.

KOON: Um hmm.

CHIN: AND WHAT DO YOU DO AT HOME?

KOON: Well, I didn't do much. [Chin laughs] But the uh. I had two chores. The morning I water my grandmother's garden. And in the evening I water her garden. The rest of the time I help around the house. Do housework. She's cooking I do little things for her, like you know, Sometimes when on holidays we make pastry. I would get up the same time she gets up. Like three in the morning. Or four in the morning. Make pastry. That's why I get up so early these days. I've always been an early riser. I wanta get up early.

CHIN: SO WHEN YOU GET UP IN THE MORNING DOES THE AIR REMIND YOU OF THE VILLAGE?

KOON: Not when I was living in the International Terrace. But here, I've only been here, like, less than two weeks. It reminds me I'll show you. [pick up and walk outside] My my uncle's uh. My uncle Back of my uncle's house is a bamboo grove. So… This is not bamboo. But…it reminds me of a bamboo grove.

CHIN: YES.

KOON: It's rectangular like that, see? It's this, you know, it's uh like you know, you know, rectangular. It's not… thick! You know what I mean?

So that reminds me of a bamboo grove. I look at that. See the little berries, red berries, in there?

CHIN: yeah.

KOON: That reminds me of the tree at school. I just finished talking about. So…down toward the whatchacallit the PEARS. And they reminds me of some fruits and fruit trees. We had a lot of fruit trees in the village. Because it's semi-tropical. We had oranges, tangerines and the bananas and all kinds of stuff. Grapes. Now the ladies grow the grapes there. Grapes in China means "po haw dee" Po hoy dee sounds like "Grandmother's children."

Your mother's mother is "PO"

CHIN: AH PAW, yeah.

KOON: "Hie dee" means children. Hie dee.

Now, in one of my poems I use "Bananas bunched together like family" you know the uh "Grapes and bananas bunched together like family" so. They grow in clusters. Then when my dad worked for somebody that exploited him, a Chinese guy, his uncle, and then he wanted to leave, you know. My... His uncle said, "Well he can go he's got so many children clinging onto him like grapes."

CHIN: RIGHT

KOON: You see the grapes cling to the vine, and they drag the vine down.

CHIN: RIGHT

KOON: What can my dad do? He's got so many things pulling him down.

CHIN: RIGHT

KOON: Children.

CHIN: YES.

KOON: Big responsibility. He's got eight children.

CHIN: WOW! Okay. Read one of your poems.

KOON: I'll read from my chapbook that I didn't show you before.

CHIN; Okay.

KOON: Some of these are more like Chinese poems. //When my cousin Sue and her family came to this country, uh. She was 19 or 18 and her sister was uh 17 - 16 and uhm my uncle my mom's younger brother, and his wife, and that uh..And two sons came also. So I was in charge of the settling in this country. I got jobs for them. I taught them English for two years.

CHIN: WOW!

KOON: I took care of all the legal the financial paperwork, everything. I even took'em to job interviews. I did everything for them. And that's why she gave her…her son to me as my godson. Henry. So I pretend I was this is was her talking when she first got to this country, and how different it is from China.

In my country, it was not like this

In my country it was not like this.

Neighbors separated by little white hospital rooms.

But one festival will flowers

paint the color of cooked shrimp.

Lychee pits the dancing eyes of children.

The warm sweet smell of water buffalo dung,

In summer ripe bananas bunched as families.

In my country I was a weaver,

a young girl with budding breasts to hide with a coarse shirt,

We did not read by tungsten light.

We read only the stars and the fireflies.

It was not guilty conversations

that receded the speed of light

but a warm river I warm in the August heat

Electric brains do not warm my blood.

But the receiving of moon cakes and the kite-flying harvest

That's pure reason a better cluck than roosters or cicadas.

The moon bathes in our cool flowing rivers,

In my burning cheeks surrender to autumn breezes,

It has mathematics the power to reverse what I lost.

It was not snow on Seven Hills. In my country as we have seen

Someone by my heart. Here cousin, take this apple.

It is the only thing I like in this paradise.

In my country, it was like this.

CHIN: HMM!

KOON: Pretend it's my uh cousin Sue that was reading that.

CHIN: RIGHT.

CHIN: YOU MENTIONED FIREFLIES. DID YOU HAVE FIREFLIES?

KOON: Yeah, I used to catch'em and put'em in a little, you know, a little medicine bottle, and carry it around. First you make a little holes in there. You know, the cap.

CHIN: I SAW FIREFLIES IN THE MIDWEST. I DON'T KNOW IT THAT'S TROPICAL OR NOT. WERE THE FIREFLIES SEASONAL?

KOON: I think so. I remember that. They were seasonal. Yeah. I think they come out after the harvest. You don't see them in the winter. But they're either spring or the fall.

CHIN: AND YOU MENTIONED THE SMELL OF BUFFALO DUNG.

KOON: Well, it's clean, you know. They eeno [only] eat grass. You know. They don't eat other things.

CHIN: RIGHT.

KOON: So they…smell clean. And we claimed them. When we see them in the village yard. They drop some dung in the village yard. We put a stick in it, and we claim it. This is ours, you know, and we use it for fertilizer.

CHIN: AHA! SO THERE WERE BUFFALO IN 1949 IN YOUR VILLAGE?

KOON: Only one!

CHIN: ooh, only one! (LAUGHS)

KOON: That was the communal buffalo. Plow…hauled the wooden plow that plowed the rice paddies for everybody.

CHIN: oh, so you didn't have tractors or

KOON: No, no. It was a family. One family was responsible for plowing. They were responsible for taking care of the one buffalo.

CHIN: AND THE WATER BUFFALO. HE OR SHE WAS WITHOUT A MATE?

KOON: Yah! In our village. I don't know what happen…with the situation in the next village, when you're a little kid you don't pay attention to everything.

CHIN: DID A BUFFALO EVER DIE?

KOON: Oh, yeah. The one we had died. Then we had to get a new cow.

CHIN: SO WHEN YOU GOT THE NEW BUFFALO IT CAME AS A CALF THEN?

KOON: // I just read that part okay? Let's see, uh.... (Reads) The water buffalo got old and died. It was shared by the whole village. Lucky money for a calf conscripted. A sad note crept into the men's drinking songs. (end read)

CHIN: WE USED TO HAVE FROGS AND I GUESS THEY CAME OUT IN THE SPRINGTIME.

KOON: Um hmm. Yah! They uh...you know. The uh. You know the gollywogs, you've seen gollywogs?

CHIN: POLLYWOGS

KOON: Pollywogs, yeah.

CHIN: DID YOU HUNT FROGS?

KOON: We fished for them. The older boys did. I was nine when I left the village. I tried, but I had no luck. What they do is they catch a little frog. They cannibals you know.

CHIN: YEAH.

KOON: Tie with string. They bob it up and down in the tall grasses. And have hold net in the other hand. So when the frog jump up and swallow it, they put the net underneath it and then take it home. That way.

CHIN: AND HOW BIG WERE THEY?

KOON: They weren't very big.

CHIN: ABOUT THAT BIG?

KOON: Maybe. At most. At most.

CHIN: AND THE LEGS WERE ABOUT THAT LONG?

KOON: Maybe, yeah. For me was more trouble than it's worth.

CHIN: YOUR GRANDMOTHER DIDN'T COOK THEM?

KOON: She did. She steamed it. You cooked the rice. You put it the on top of the rice. Then uh steamed it that way, yeah.

CHIN: WOULD SHE STEAM THE WHOLE FROG, OR DID SHE STEAM JUST THE LEGS?

KOON: Well she…She'd clean it. Clean the gut out. And then steam the whole thing, yeah.

CHIN: THE HEAD DOO? WE ALWAYS THREW AWAY THE HEAD.

KOON: I don't remember. That. I don't remember. I don't particularly like to eat frogs.

CHIN: (LAUGHS)

KOON: Every once in awhile they eat you can get'em in Chinatown.

CHIN: YEAH.

Koon: Yeah. I like to eat bigger things. Chicken. We had chicken in the house.

CHIN: Oh, in the house.

KOON: Yeah, in the house. We had a…the house was a duplex. The house was like this. Here's the entrance here. And here's the kitchen, here. Here's the bedroom here. And there's a door which we can lock from outside. And here's the utility room shared by both duplex owners. In the utility room, there's a drain here. The uh the uh… the roof is open, that part of it. Cuz the monsoon, you know, you don't want any water to collect too heavily on your roof.

CHIN: RIGHT.

KOON: It could damage your roof. So we just let the water just drop right down, and drain underneath the house. We had the farm implements there. ( ) any implements. The next door neighbor, who was my father's cousin's mother, they lived there.

CHIN: WHAT WERE THE FARM IMPLEMENTS?

KOON: Just hoes. Shovels. Little things. Ordinary gardening.

CHIN: WERE THEY MANUFACTURED OR …

KOON: They were manufactured. There was a town nearby. A small town. They call it Sir Bo Huey. Our district is called Sir Bo. We just go into town and buy your little. Buy hardware items and medicine and things like that.

CHIN: SO UH . WHAT TIME OF DAY WOULD YOU GO TO TOWN? WOULD IT TAKE ALL DAY TO GO TO TOWN?

KOON: Where we are, just like about a fifteen minute walk…ten fifteen minute walk, yeah.

CHIN: WOULD YOU GO ALONE?

KOON: Oh, you can go alone. It's completely safe for children at that time.

CHIN: WOULD YOU GO WITH A BUNCH OF CHILDREN, FOR FUN?

KOON: Sometimes. It. On special occasion we go there for fun. You know like uh. We never did like…After a heavy rain, you know, like uh. Sometimes the river gets, you know swollen up. We like to go watch the river. We like to watch people fishing with the net, you know. They uh they lift the net. Tied to a big bamboo pole, you know, and the net's like this you know, they lift it. They wait for awhile. Then bait some fishes, maybe they put a fish head in it or something in the net or something. Fishnet they just lift it up.

CHIN: SO IT'S A NET AND WHEN THEY PUT IT DOWN IT BUTTERFLIES OUT,

KOON: Yes.

CHIN: AND THEN WHEN THEY LIFT IT UP, THE WINGS…FOLD IN.

KOON: Yeah, it doesn't completely fold in, so that, so just lift all the water so the fish cannot jump back in.

CHIN: WHAT KIND OF FISH?

KOON: I don't remember now. They all kinds of little ones, like uh. There's carp. There's dace. Dee eeh cee eeh. There's uh I just know the uh. I just remember there's a catfish.There's probably something like perch, you know things like that. There's there are freshwater fish where we were.

CHIN: CATFISH ARE BOTTOMFEEDER

KOON: Yeah.

CHIN: PERCH ARE BOTTOMFEEDERS TOO.

KOON: They eat the shrimp that eat feed off the seaweed, in the ocean, anywhere. I don't know what it is with the freshwater perch.

CHIN: AS THEY GOT BIGGER DID THE TASTE OF THE FISH CHANGE?

KOON: Yeah, Yeah. Yeah.

CHIN: AND TASTE MORE MUDDY

KOON: You mean catfish and carp. After a certain size of carp people don't eat'em.

CHIN: THIS IS A STUPID QUESTION. WERE THERE SUPERSTITIONS ABOUT THE FISH?

KOON: Ah, let's see. Carp is supposed to be uh you know you see all these Chinese uh greetings, you know uh papers? The carp is supposed to be longe…longevtivity.

CHIN: LONGEVITY, YES.

KOON: Yeah, longevity. Ah. Ah. Catfish. I don't know what that is. I don't think there's anything related to catfish. You know, that reminds me of poem. Not a poem but a story.

There's two kinds of fish. I can only say in Chinese I don't know what they are in English. Dot....Dot nguy, tiyew nguy....Dot nguy tiyew nguy." One of it's catfish and one is say carp, okay? Two fish at the in the uh. Supposedly this guy uh said he could know everything. I mean he uh he could, you know, find out, you know by uh uh sixth sense whe...where everything is. So the...

The king! Heard about that. I mean.... He was a con-artist or something like that okay? So the king...the emperor heard about that, and the emperor, something along. The story, and the emperor's gold or something valuable, that belong to the emperor.

So the emperor heard about this guy, so he uh. He sent two guys to conscript him to go the palace. Uh you know...Use his sixth sense to recover his loot or whatever it was.

So these two uh I don't know what you call'em...soldiers? Or whatever they call them. So he brought this...bring in this guy to the palace. So along the way, this guy saw a pond. It was being dried up.

And there was two fish in the bottom of , you know, the mud. So obviously the water's gonna be, you know, evaporating and they'll die there. Just two fish.

So he so...So he says...So this guy the uh the seer, right? He says, then well, he was making the comment about himself. He says uh. When he was talking to the fish, he says uh, "Ah dot yut say. Ah tiew yut say. Nay say yeh gong wooey." Which means the Dot fish will die, the Tiew fish will die. They'll both die before I will."

However that Dot and Tiew were the surnames of those two soldiers. So they said, "Maybe he does know! He can predict, you know, what's going on."

So they got scared. You know how they kowtow on the ground? "Please, we'll help you." They the one's that stole the valuables. They said, "We think we'll them back to the emperor. Just don't tell'm who stole it. We'll concoct a plan to give it back to the emperor."

So, he goes back there. Says, "Oh, yeah. It's hidden. I don't know who stole them, it's hidden. The emperor get it back, so (he) declared amnesty.

But the poetry is this, "Ah Dot yut say. Ah Tiew yat say. Nay say ah gong wooey." Which means, in Toisahnese, is "The fish will die before the speaker says." But another interpretation....another translation, he said, "They are staying because he will carve it to happen." Because he know he stole they stoled it. It's accidental that the language is like that. You see what I mean?

CHIN: ALMOST

KOON: You know Chinese have a lot of homonyms. The Chinese language because it only has so many characters. It cannot create new words like the English alphabet. You know, just make the word longer, right? You have a new word. They can create many many new words in the English language.

But Chinese have so many characters, so they double up meanings for each character. So they all have the same sound, even though they have different tones. So they have a lot of homonyms. A lot of the words sound the same, but they have a lot of different meanings.

So that's what in this case, what he just said sounds like something else. So these guys uh meant thought he meant something *else.* So they thought he knew they'd stolen it. And they confessed to him. So that's what happened.

CHIN: RIGHT. UH. THE BUFFALO THAT DIED.

KOON: yes.

CHIN: DID YOU EAT IT?

KOON: Yeah. That was the custom. It was shared by the whole village. And everybody who ate it contributed money for the new calf.

CHIN: WHAT DID TASTE LIKE?

KOON: It was tough. You probably have to cook it, you know chop, you know, mince it up, and chop it and steam it, or something. Cook it with that turnip or something.

CHIN: WHAT DO THEY CALL THAT?

KOON: Ngoy choy. Mooey choy.

My grandmother like to chop up the beef really…mince it. She steam it with mooey choy, you know. For me. Yeah. We very seldom eat beef. We're not in a grazing area. You know, we just have to, we…we raise pigs and chickens and fish.

CHIN: HOW DEEP WAS YOUR POND?

KOON: Yeah. Yeah. It increased in depth. It was not a vee shape. Parabolic shape. It was over somebody's head. We raised fish in it. It was fed by underground water. Maybe the same water as the well water. So there was a cool stream of water going into the pond.

And there was a drainage. To drain into a little creek, and if flows into the river.

CHIN: AND YOU SAID WHEN IT FLOODED IN THE MONSOON FISH WOULD GET INTO THE POND.

KOON: Also trapped in rice paddies too.

CHIN: OKAY. IT'S AFTER 3: YOU'RE BACK FROM SCHOOL. YOU'VE HELPED YOUR GRANDMOTHER.

KOON: Yeah.

CHIN: IS IT GETTING DARK?

KOON: OH WE HAVE SUPERSTITIONS. GHOSTS. Oh, we have superstitions. Ghosts. Everybody's claimed they've seen a ghost. I never. But a lot people claimed tey've seen a ghost.

CHIN: HOW DO YOU OCCUPY YOUR TIME, YOU WATCH TV?

KOON; No tv. No radio. No bicycles. No running water. No electricity. No books to speak of. Just schoolbooks. Didn't even have paper. Wrote everything on a slate. And an abacus that I you know, you know kids don't to study. Don't like to practice.

Just play in the village yard. Games you know like jacks, you know with uh little rocks. I used to play jacks. Play uh kickball, our version of soccer, you know like in the village yard. Hide and seek when we're really small.

Swimming. Physical activity. Little kids climb trees. Make things out of bamboo. Popguns out of bamboo.

CHIN: DID YOU HAVE SNAKES?

KOON: Yeah, We had snakes. We had regular garter snakes and these innocuous snakes. But but we had water snakes. They're poisonous. They swim on top the water. They're really scary. And their really swift. Swim right on top the water. Course they're not on every pond. Where they are we don't go near them.

//The pond where we swam didn't have snakes we were careful. There are grown up, "These ponds off limits." You know, you don't go to that pond. Not to swim anyway. Go to go fishing. We don't go swimming there.

And they all say that the uh if somebody's dies in a pond that's bad luck to swim there.

CHIN: DID YOU HAVE SNAKEHUNTING PARTIES?

KOON: NO. You know some people make a profession to catch snakes and sell them. You know. For food. I guess the restaurants you know restaurants in snake call'em the snakemeat. I've never had snakemeat. It just never appealed to me.

CHIN: WHAT WAS YOUR FAVORITE MEAL?

KOON: You know when I was a little boy my favorite food was pigs feet stewed in rice vinegar. Sweet rice vinegar. With peanuts and lotus needles.

CHIN: TOMORROW I'M GOING TO SEE ASSUNTA.

//

CHIN: THERE IS NO SUCH SAYING IN CHINESE AS "THE WORTH OF A WOMAN IS MEASURED BY THE LOUDNESS OF HER HUSBAND'S BELCH." BECAUSE WOMEN ALSO EAT. AND BELCH AND SLURP.

I think what they're trying to say is the uh Chinese culture is chauvinistic. All that crap. I tell you in my family. My mom worked right alongside my dad. Doing dishes and chores he did, in restaurants, and then she goes home and take care of the kids. And she has a garden besides.

In the village you know. Although my grandmother's feet was bound she was part of the aristocracy. After the Japanese came, they were poor. They bombed the distillery, bombed the store. The reduced everything to rubbles. She had to work. She had to be a peasant. Feet that look like a common ginger. She took care of me. She loved more than my own parents did.

She had to work in the rice paddies. She grew her vegetables. She made pastries to give to a few kids.

CHIN: There are several books by whites about the agonies suffered by women with bound feet. Did your grandmother ever complain about her bound feet?

KOON: Well see at that time when the feet were bound, they're considered the part of the upper class. "A woman's worth" in terms of a dowry. A "Curtain Marriage" , means marrying for money for position, that was worth more but in her family what that means, she was not to do peasant work. So her family could afford it. So at that time you remember China is a feudal country. So that was a feudal practice. Okay.

Do we complain about King Arthur and his practices? No, we don't. That was the historical times. That's what was believed at that time. That was the socio-economic conditions at that time. I mean that's how…how…you know the evolution was at that time the socio-economic system. But we don't complain about that. I mean we do, but we don't. You see what I mean? We have to put everything in context.

We take things out of context. But because the revolution in China, the foreign invasions, and so forth, people have to work even if their feet have been bound. So of course she would not walk as well as somebody whose feet were not bound.

CHIN: DID SHE LOOSEN THE BINDINGS?

KOON: Oh yeah. Loosened the bindings. But it looks like a common ginger. The toes overlap each other.

It's like in this country if you're born poor, you're down in the ghetto and you need the money to live. And you commit a crime. You go to prison. Twenty years later they release you. Well,, you're gonna have that mark on you. That you've been to prison. So they ask you where have you been? What jobs do you held in the last twenty years?

It's the same kind of thing. Social stigma.

CHIN: HOW OLD WAS YOUR GRANDMOTHER DID SHE COME OVER HERE?

KOON: No, we couldn't. … It costs money to bring somebody over here. You have to support them, see? She was old, and by the time I came, she was in her sixties. So, the uh…you know…She would not be productive in terms of making money. And we as a family of ten people with one include income. And that was being a frycook. Imagine one frycook supporting ten people. So we lived in the housing projects. So here's something I tellya. When I was fourteen. My dad was a partner in a house of prostitution. And I had to help him out. The front…the cover of the place was a restaurant. I had to help work there after school when I was fourteen years old.

I worked there Friday, Saturdays, and Sundays. Work until three in the morning. That could be explain one of the reasons I have mental problems. I did not have a regular childhood in this country.

And another thing was we had some, you know, …problems, with some people when I was fourteen. And my dad took me aside, says, "The gun is in the dresser. So, somebody tries to come in the window you shoot'em."

CHIN: HMM. WHAT TOWN WAS THIS?

KOON: Aberdeen, Washington. And the sheriff, you know. Years later, the sheriff comes to the restaurant. He says, "I Wanta see your dad."

I said, "Well, my dad's asleep now. So, I don't want to bother him."

So he gets real mad at me, you know. Real mad at me. Cuz I didn't know the connection. I didn't know he was getting paid off for things my dad was doing. I didn't know he was getting paid off for things my dad was doing. See Iwas very naïve, you know. The Chinese have the uh monkey, uh you know uh don't see, monkey don't hear, monkey don't talk. That's the Chinese saying.

CHIN: HOW MANY GIRLS DID YOUR FATHER AND HIS PARTNER RUN?

KOON: Well actually it was run by a madam. She was half Mexican. Her name was Sally. There were three girls that were actors. Ginger, Lee, and Suzy. I remember their names.

CHIN: WERE THEY CHINESE?

KOON: No, they were white girls. See my dad and I the restaurant was called the China Doll Restaurant in Montesano, Washington. Back in 1960… well I was in the fourth…the 7th grade so I was 14. I came here. See, I was born in 49, so I was 14, so it'd be round 1963 or 64 around there.

So I used to have to take the bus p to school to go to Montesano ten miles away, and start working after school.

And work till three or four in the morning. My dad drive me home, and then. I couldn't sleep. You know, because of all the tension.

And my brothers and sister began waking up early in the morning. You know, I've been going… Come Sunday. I go out into the woods by myself. Everything would be pitch black. I couldn't see nothing. That's how bad it was.

I somehow I just supressed it. I forgot all about it. Then became the star pupil at school. I don't know why.

My dad didn't want me to join these clubs or turn out for sports after school. Although I was asked to turn out for swimming. You know, just my dad, you know like the president of the literary club in high school. I had one meeting after school. My dad said, "Where've you been?"

I says, "I been… Had a meeting of the literary club."

He says, "From now on, you come directly home. You have a family and eight children. I can't do it all buy myself. You gotta help me. So you come directly home."

That's when I realized the uh what kind of burden he had. But you know, but he wanted me to uh to follow his footsteps. He had six sons. So. My dad is one of those Confucian guys. He wanta impart back to six sons, right? So he wanted me to be uh you know. Take over his restaurant someday and expand the business.

He took me to the bank after he came back from the University of Oregon. And he took me to talk to the bank manager. The manager says, "Yeah, I can give you credit for a hundred thou."

A hundred thousand dollars back in 1971's a lot of money! And my dad says, "See, the manager trusts us. You don't have to get an apartment. If you don't like the restaurant business you can go into real estate.

My dad was actively sabotaging my car…college career.

CHIN: HOW BIG WAS HE? WAS HE TALLER THAN YOU?

KOON: Yeah, he was 5' 8". He's a musc…not muscular. He was athletic. He was the captain of the San Francisco Chinatown volley ball team. Yeah, he was the number one kung fu guy in the village. He carried the first flag.

CHIN: SO HE WAS A MEMBER OF A TONG?

KOON: Well he's a member of one Triad. I don't know how many triad's there are. They claim there are 26 triads in Hong Kong. The last time I heard, there might be hundreds now. There might be hundreds in China.

The triads were started to overthrow the Manchurian dynasty. But I saw reference they chart it back to Li Po (700 ad).

CHIN: AT THE WHOREHOUSE. WERE YOU INITIATED BY ONE OF THE GIRLS?

KOON: No. No. I was 14. I wanted to, but you know but. 6:59 AMhe girl that I liked the best was Suzy. She was 20. She helped me wash dishes, after after we close. I was dead tire. You know I get up at about 6-7 in the morning, work till three in the morning washing dishes. By hand at that time. She helped me wash dishes. I liked her quite a bit. She was nice.

The other girls. They had troubles. The cops start coming in. The madams you know uh… "Well it's too hot in here. It's too cold in here."

My dad says, "Oh, she's taking too much drugs." Then there's people that come in, says, "Oh, I'm the mayor of this town." "No, I'm the sheriff of this town." You never know who they are. They're drinking. They have the bar there. You know, never know.

And they come right through the kitchen they go upstairs the backstairs to the upstairs.

CHIN: HOW MANY PEOPLE WERE IN THE KITCHEN?

KOON: Just me and my dad. We have to take care of like, I don't know…60 you know 60 customers. Maybe 60 –80 customers. I don't know. I mean my dad was always shouting me. You know, like "Get this thing done! Quick responsible. I'm waiting for this. I'm waiting for this."

Can you imagine that? I've only been here for two years two and half years, and I don't know English. I'm getting shout at. And the uh you know…

CHIN: SO SIXTY CUSTOMERS. WERE THEY FOR THE WHOREHOUSE OR THE RESTAURANT?

KOON: Some was for the whorehouse and some for the restaurant. Some don't even know it's a whorehouse.

CHIN:

KOON: Well actually I thought that my dad was just work for the madame as an employee. But actually later on just recently I figure, well he was actually a partner.

The madame got run out of town. She called my dad from somewhere she claims she was working for Bob Hope. She wanted my dad to work for her.

Who knows? You can't trust those people.

CHIN: WAS SHE A GOOD LOOKING WOMAN?

KOON: No she was in her 50's. And half Mexican. She wasn't good looking.

But I know why she was run out of town.

The first thing she gave me when she closed shop. She gave me a tape recorder. She was blackmailing people.

CHIN: AHH!

KOON: That's why she was run out of town. If you pay off the cops, pay off the mayor, you won't get run out of town. Even though the people complain. But if you're blackmailing people you get run out of town. She got greedy, in other words.

CHIN: YES.

KOON: Aberdeen is known for prostitution in the old days.

CHIN: WHAT DID YOUR FATHER DRESS LIKE?

KOON: THE ONLY COMPLIMENT I EVER GOT FROM MY MOTHER WAS, "HE DRESS LIKE AN HONEST MAN." Losut. Not a showoff. Honest. Just like you, the way you dress.

CHIN: WOMEN?

Well I had this Japanese girlfriend when I came to Seattle. I met her at the Last Exit, as a matter of fact. Japanese American, she was born here. I was 20. I had a couple of girls after that, but nobody was a really…most of it's in my book. Nobody was…well I had some bad luck. I couldn't afford to support anybody. Cuz of my mental illness.

I had a dream which was to be a mathematician. And I was 28 years old I was hospitalized and I realized I could never be a mathematician.

Well there's one I met in the hospital. She was really. She was from Hong Kong and she worked for when you get visas, would that be the consulate, the Hong Kong consulate.

The Love this abode contains….

We have lived in 32 abodes, Susana, red brick, four square,

Nearly a palace, or 32 pages of thin paper, a small book.

And in each story, there's an abode of red brick, inside

Which are a set of 32 books, and the love each book contains

Is more solid than a red brick, and four squares together make

A foundation, and so, Susanna, why did you say our love

Cannot exist in paper or fenced by red brick, and is that why

You sold jewelry because you were convinced it was good jewelry.

And stamped visas because we needed more investments in Hong Kong?

Now I'm alone in a single abode of wood and iron nails,

And lone and lonely the cold air seeps and my pen fails.

And, Susanna, where are you since the hospital in 1993?

Should I print your last name and shame your father, who took you

Out to drink with his buddies on the eve of the Chinese New Year?

And wanted to know if I coud get SSI if I went with you

To PSU? Where I would live and you would annotate my mishaps

In your sociology book; and I would tell you everything about

"Michellle," the woman you were so jealous of, and asked me

Is it true. It's half true, Susanna, and only half, for half of us

Live in abode s of paper and half of us live in abodes of brick,

And where the truth is, Susanna, is underneath your left breast.

Where you let me put my right palm in the hospital, because

That's where your heart is...

CHIN: WE'RE BACK ON THE FARM. IT'S TIME TO GO TO BED. WHO SAYS IT'S TIME TO GO TO BED?

KOON: Well, first of all. You can't see anymore. So you have to light up the kerosene lamp. That costs money for the kerosene. If you don't have money they won't let you in again. You have food and have to barter food, for items like cough (?) We could sell things for a little bit of money. But mainly we depended the money from my parents, overseas. But we had kerosene lamp. We try to get to bed as soon as we can. So my grandmother would feed me some cod liver oil. Rinse it down with some boiled hot water. In the winter that does two things. That keep you warm while you fall asleep with the hot water. And the other thing is that the. It rinse down the cod liver oil.

We sleep with all the clothes on, and socks too. Cuz there's no indoor heating. So we sleep with all the blankets we have. And I slept with my grandmother until I was eleven years old.

CHIN: OH, SO YOU SLEPT IN THE SAME BED?

KOON: It's not a strange a custom. Even kids would sleep with the mother until they're eleven twelve years old.

The only thing that I remember vividly is cicadas. Cuz they make a lot of noise. We try to catch'em with uh stick stuff with a long babmboo pole and just get'em stuck on it. They roast them. They eat'em, you know.

CHIN: WHAT'D THEY TASTE LIKE?

KOON: How'd they taste? Kinda burnt.

Memoir 1105

From #1105 = 5 x 13 x 17 an apartment in the high rise you can see quite a few things. Including the night when the firemen washed the blood off the street on South Main Street and 6th Ave. South in Seattle Chinatown. They spent the longest time to hose the blood down. As usual Donnie Chin got there first before the firemen came and in my delusional state, I wonder if he had something to do with the stabbing or killing or whatever that happened, because it never made it to the newspapers. Since I was trained as a worst-case-scenario analyst I assume it was a homicide, because it happened at the very place that a few years earlier a fire department official was knifed to death by a mentally ill man that they had just released from jail. These things happened between the years 1996 and 2008 when I was illegally removed from there. I lived in Chinatown for over 20 years and things are still opaque.

Sometime before that Paul Allen erected his building on 5th Avenue South, which blocked my view to the waterfront. And subsequently buildings to the left of his obstructed my view from the 11th floor to the West Seattle Bridge, which is like an onramp to infinity. One may make note that the football stadium was constructed as the aftermath of the Kingdome implosion. It was an acknowledgement to Paul Allen's interest in keeping a world-class football team in Seattle and so despite having a measure to fund the stadium partly with public money defeated in the day time in the state legislature, it was voted again after midnight and our illustrious governor Gary Locke presided over the vote in favor of Paul Allen's public concern for vicarious mayhem and sports gambling.

When the Korean night club was operating, sometimes it pours out in the street where drunken young people and high on something mill around my building's intersection and it is quite spooky having over 50 or more drunken people arguing and trying to prolong a party. One time the cops busted the place. That was the time I hear the order some police vehicle amplified out, "Walk backwards with your hands up." Then I saw an undercover cop came out of the club and was hugged by a female cop.

Fat Aunt

He rang the doorbell hard. Eventually a woman pushed the door curtain a crack and looked out. Opening the door, she spoke, "You here already? Where is luggage?" He looked at her short rotund body in sweats, her face is catfish-like; she is shorter and fatter than he remembers of her seven years ago.

"It is at the Greyhound station," he answered her question almost involuntarily.

"So, if you don't like Fat Aunt, you just go back to Aberdeen, eh?" Expecting no answer, she tells him to follow her upstairs. "Be careful of Buddha figurines on steps," she admonishes, "they worth money." He made a mental image of someone escaping a fire and tumbling down the stairs because of tripping over the figurines. *Money can cost you your life,* he thought to himself.

Two weeks earlier in Seattle he got a call from his father telling him of his cousin Martin's funeral. His father told him to come home immediately. He took the Greyhound home. His father told him what had happened.

"Martin got out of corrections, found his girl friend shacking up with a Wah Ching," his father begins to relate what he had heard from the Old Guy Benny. Apparently, Benny went down to San Francisco and questioned the guy who killed Martin. Martin had in a fit of jealousy climbed through his rival's window at night armed with a knife. As he approached the sleeping couple, his ex-girlfriend screamed. The new lover grabbed his gun from under his pillow and shot Martin in the neck. Martin kept coming. The new boyfriend shot him again in the neck. Incredible as it seemed, Martin was still upright and kept coming. Two more rapid shots to the neck finally put him down. Benny told my father, "It was self-defense. There is nothing we can do."

His father then said, "You go and keep your Aunt company. She is lonely now her youngest son died."
So, he came to stay with his Aunt as a matter of family obligation. Fat Aunt put him in Martin's room.

The minute he stepped into Martin's room, he had a peculiar sense that it reeked of hyper-masculinity.
In the semi-darkness the first thing he noticed was a black panther figurine on the dresser, a stack of Hustler on the foot of the bed and a Bruce Lee poster with chucks on the wall. But he was so tired he immediately crashed onto the bed and slept.

In the middle of the night, Fat Aunt roused him from his sleep. "I want you make phone call for me to Hong Kong," Fat Aunt ordered, "It is mid afternoon there now and I am looking for a boy to claim for a godson so he keep Martin's memory alive." Fat Aunt was all business, like the boss of two sweatshops she was. The nephew had spent some time in Hong Kong and knew that it was "funny business." Nevertheless, he dialed the number Fat Aunt gave him and handed the phone over to her.

"You go back to Aberdeen now and go back school in Seattle. I don't need you now. I will have someone honor memory of my son. Since the nephew was born in China, he knew something was in the works but he doesn't ask. He is a mathematics student. And he is also a philosophy student. He quoted Wittgenstein to himself, "Whereof one can speak, thereof must one speak clearly, and whereof one cannot speak, thereof must one remain silent. *All I know is that it costs money to make a telephone call to Hong Kong*, he thought to himself, *and all I did was to dial a number which I knew nothing about.*

Jose Again

Here is a man who has traveled and lived on three continents, only to die alone in a desolate North American hotel room. Not that he didn't have family; families he had two of his own, one in Hong Kong and one in Peru. But his spouses only gave him illegitimate children.

My uncle Jose always leaves a trail of water and bits of vegetables when he worked in the restaurant kitchen. Similarly, he left unfinished business and traces of himself where he had traveled and lived. He walked unevenly because one of his legs was shorter than the other. Born in China, immigrated to Peru at an early age, and came to Washington State when sponsored by his sister at the age of fifty, he died alone in a hotel room meant for an overnight guest in Seattle's Chinatown. Is there something that attracted people to come to Seattle's Chinatown, a most comatose place in the entire cosmos, or is it simply bad *feng shui*?

When Jose first arrived, he and I shared the old house on Bay Avenue, across the dirt field beyond which lies the rail tracks. Freights with cargo came from Georgia on the Georgia Pacific line to the Port of Grays Harbor in Aberdeen, where in the past, lumber was shipped to Japan. In exchange of lumber to build houses in earthquake-ridden Japan, we purchased the latest in consumer electronic gadgets from there.

My mother is Jose's younger sister. When our small family-owned café in the small town of Aberdeen expanded when tourism was still good, my father needed an extra hand in the kitchen. So we sponsored Jose over from Peru. Jose claimed to have worked in big *chifas* in Peru that served over a thousand people. After some familiarity with her oldest brother, whom she has not seen since she was six in China, my mother, between dinner and bar rush, would say, "Take back your wife, Poi's mother, so that you will have someone to take care of you in old age and burn incense for you in *the after.*"

"But I didn't adopt Poi," Jose would protest, "That woman did herself," referring to his legal wife in China.

"It is too late to argue such matters," my mother would speak a bit louder over the cracking of the hot oil in the frying wok, "Your foreign Peru woman is a foreign devil. At least your wife in China is Chinese." To this Jose had no reply. He was over fifty with a limp and dependent on his sister's family for work and company. None of them were sympathetic to his life's choices. And Jose couldn't speak English, although fluent in Chinese and Spanish.

The night that Jose died in his room at the Republic Hotel in Chinatown, Doctor Hong signed Jose's death certificate. His Peruvian wife Carmen said that she and my uncle Jose went shopping the previous day and Jose had fallen on the escalator. That's why his body was all bruised up. My mother didn't pay for the funeral and burial and so Jose got a pauper's grave. I didn't even know which cemetery. My mother had not talked to me for some time and I found out about Jose's death from my brother Lange. Lange is the bearer of bad news, as well as good news, I suppose, because he is the bearer of all news. That was his function in the family. He had the gift of gab. The rest of us did whatever work was in front of us - chopping onion, de-veining prawns, whipping gravy, or ladling soup. Lange had polio in one arm and so he waited on the customers. Since none of us got paid when we worked for our family in our teen years, Lange worked for tips. So, Lange became a "smooth talker," as our family friend Marvin the Sears and Roebuck mechanic would say.

He spins it just right is the way I saw how he operated. My sister Linda said that Lange was just "happy-go-lucky." My siblings all seem to speak a different language than I did, because I was born in China, the same as my parents. My parents referred to my siblings as "jook sing" or bamboo-natured, because they were like bamboo, hard and sturdy outside, but wildly hollow inside. So, I got the burden of being the Number-One-Son. It is just some unfair game my parents played on guys like Jose and me.

"I don't know how much professor makes, I make thirty thou," is what my father says to me. I had wanted to be a mathematician ever since I saw an inspirational film about a mathematician and how goes about doing his work. The film showed a mathematician; just a man dressed casually bending over a creek and looking intently at the flow of the water. He then draws arrows on his clipboard and scribbled some letters and numbers. He is representing the water flow by a vector field. These are a bunch of short arrows that depict the direction and force of the water flow. This way he could calculate the erosion on the creek bank over time. He makes a representation of the real world with a set of diagrams and formulas. He just needed a clipboard and a pen. I thought to myself, "Wow, that's a job I like - work alone, anywhere, see things out there and inside your head. And you don't have to be in a shop or an office. That would be the ideal job for me!" And I did well in high school. But my father had other plans for me and was out to sabotage me. At least, that's what my paranoia ideation tells me now. Today I am 62 years old and my father has been dead for 25 years, a quarter of a century. And my wife tells me that I am still talking about my father as though he was in the bedroom with us. But what my parents did tell me though, one night after the closing hour of the restaurant, they took out a jade and gold set. It was an investment. They are from the old country and never trust the value of currency and so they invested in jewelry. And the Chinese value jade the most.

My mother holds up a jade bracelet. Even I was surprised at the color composition of the jade. It appeared to be milkfish with different hues of different colors diffusing in the stone, as if an orange or blue cloud would disperse and spread in the sky. "You hold up a piece of jade to the sky," my mother said, "it is looks like clouds running in the jade, then it is good jade," she said.

"Someday when we can't see you anymore, you will have some jade too," said my dad. He was wearing a soft green sweater, as if that softened him as well. That was a benign time when I was 21 years old, back from the University of Oregon, visiting for the Christmas holiday. Later on times did not prove to be so bucolic.

The Proprietress of Love

"Something there is making my heart empty."
She is fond of divulging.

My Uncle pens firmly from China, "Ai mo nung tsor (love to but unable to help)." As Lorca in his somnambular ballad, "Mocito, si yo puedo, este
trado estaba cerraba, per yo no soy yo, y ni mi casa es ya mi casa (If I am able, young man, this bargain would be closed, but I am no longer I and neither is my house my house)."

The cracks in the sidewalk are not a match for this day of thunder in the sky, the sixth day of the storm season, and the wind forebodes downed power lines, like the pain of jilted love.

She is fond of giving me her hand, when no customers are in the store and says, "Look how fast my hands are aging!" I cast a lazy glance toward the videos of love, and say, I can, I can manage you. And as she smiles, a customer walks in.

I return often when either she or I need a boost from each other.

Somewhere hidden in the city Mr. Five Willows is staring at the computer screen, with a glass of wine within reach, and as he pours from the bottle to refill the glass, a sudden downpour of rain outside.
It is too early to trust the weather.

At the barbecue shop a man purchases a roast duck, cleaved and boxed by "the chop-chop man," who laments he is not an old "wah queue (long-time immigrant)." His cleaver swings up and chops down all day long, and no, this is not a persistent mirage.

Someone is eating with oily lips tonight. Someone who is already fat.

Mr. Schuler and the Triple-L

"Do you need help with going to the bathroom?" he asked.

"No," I answered. This was the first of a series of questions that I didn't feel like replying to, as it was cold and austere in his office.

"Do you have any dietary restrictions?"

I didn't like the word "restrictions" and so I said "No." The snow was drifting down outside the window. I had lug my suitcase from the road to this compound because the taxi couldn't drive in the unshoveled snow. It was a bad year in Seattle. The worst snow in 20 years. But the hospital paid for the cab.

"You know," Mr. Schuler peered over his steel-rimmed glasses, "Mr. Woon, I think you are a smart man. You can think your way through troubles, and so I don't think you will be here too long."

The space heaters made a clicking sound. The heater was trying to come on, but it rather sounded like Morse or military codes. And Mr. Schuler was not a literary figure but a former colonel in the Air Force.

"Do you have a will?"

I did not answer. Such a question is not culturally-sensitive.

"Do you have a will?"

He asked again. His had suddenly looked very large.

"I am very tired," I feigned in a weak voice. Can we do this interview at a later time. Now I do need to go to the bathroom.

"You will do just fine here. I am thinking of putting you to work here. Being part of the scheme of things will make you feel more at home here." He then "volunteered" me to help the breakfast cook to wash dishes.

"You won't be here very long," he repeated. He picked up the phone, and a few minutes later Andy came and led me to my cottage.

I saw three beds in my room, one of the three rooms in the cottage. I peered into another room where the television sound bites were coming from. I saw three motley men sitting at the edge of their beds, each watching to a separate tv. I thought, "Oh shit, here is where I am going to be, waiting for Godot."

But then I remember what the Colonel had said, "You won't be here very long."

I saw that in the alcove there was a little table with a jigsaw puzzle in progress.

I sat there for a moment. I looked out the window. I was in my winter jacket and the cottage was unheated. The snow was drifting down. It was 4 pm or so, but it was already getting dark and the white snowflakes drifts and drifts down, and some of them landed in the crotch of a birch tree.

I realized finally I was at the Triple L. I was not in a hurry to meet my fellow residents. I took out my journal. This was going to be a serious writers' retreat.

About the author:

Koon Woon (1949 -) was born Locke Kau Koon in Nan On village in Guangdong Province in China and he immigrated to the US in 1960 to Aberdeen, WA. He grew up working in the family restaurant and attended high school in Aberdeen before attending the University of Washington to study mathematics and philosophy. As events unfold, mental illness played havoc in his life. He is thankful of all the help he received to cope with his condition and situation. This book is a slice of his non-ordinary life in which he pays tribute to his forebears who came to this land "when rails were young."

This book is generously supported by a grant from the City of Seattle's Office of Arts & Culture, and special thanks is given to my project manager Irene Gomez.

Made in the USA
Charleston, SC
13 May 2016